EDUCATED UNEMPLOYED YOUTH IN NAGALAND: A SOCIOLOGICAL STUDY

EDUCATED UNEMPLOYED YOUTH IN NAGALAND: A Sociological Study

KEDILEZO KIKHI

AKANSHA PUBLISHING HOUSE
NEW DELHI

AKANSHA PUBLISHING HOUSE
4649-B/21, Ansari Road
Darya Ganj, New Delhi - 110 002
Email: ektabooks@yahoo.com
Ph. : 23263193 / 9811582579

Educated Unemployed Youth in Nagaland:
A Sociological Study

First Published 2006

ISBN 81-8370-055-1

[The responsibility for the facts stated, conclusions reached etc. is entirely that of the Author. The publisher is not responsible for them, whatsoever.]

PRINTED IN INDIA

Published by M.P. Misra for Akansha Publishing House, New Delhi and Printed at Tarun Offset Press, Delhi.

Foreword

The unabated rise of educated unemployed all over the country and more particularly in a small state like Nagaland is causing great concern for the planners and the public alike. Thousands of educated unemployed youth in the state are forced to confront with the harsh reality of unemployment against which they have no defenses. The problem of unemployment among the educated Naga youth is a serious problem which needs timely attention and solution.

The **Educated Unemployed in Nagaland: A Sociological Study** is a modified version of the doctoral thesis by Dr. Kedilezo Kikhi at the Department of sociology, NEHU, Shillong. Dr. Kedilezo Kikhi being a Naga Sociologist from Kohima has a first hand experience on the problems of the unemployed youth particularly at the Kohima town from which he hails.

In this book Dr. Kedi attempts to address some of the key questions pertaining to educated unemployed youth in Nagaland, such as: What is the magnitude and extent of educated unemployment? What are the aspirations and expectations of educated job seekers? What is the probability of an unemployed person to get a job in the state? Are the educated worried about getting a job? How do they view the job market? What is the frequency of job attempts? What are the various problems that beset the unemployed youth and the related social consequences? What is their attitude towards the government with regard to the method of selection to various jobs, the employment exchanges and the present educational system? What is the opinion of the educated youth towards various self-employment schemes?

I am sure this volume will help the administrators and the planners in formulating policies to meet the challenge of unemployed youth in the state and also it will certainly provide some basic background material to the research scholars and I wish this finds a wider readership cutting across the policy makers, activists, Nagaland watchers as well as academia.

C JOSHUA THOMAS
Acting Director
ICSSR-NERC
Shillong-793 014

Acknowledgements

This volume is the revised version of the doctoral dissertation submitted to the Department of Sociology, North Eastern Hill University (NEHU), Shillong. The author has done his research work on ***A Sociological Study of Educated Unemployed Youth of Kohima Town of Nagaland*** under the supervision of Professor C. Nunthara.

I am deeply indebted to Professor C. Nunthara for the patience and the great pain he took in supervising and guiding me at every phase of my research work. He has been a source of knowledge, inspiration and encouragement to me throughout my research work.

I would like to express my thanks to my beloved teachers at NEHU, Professors A.C. Sinha, M.N. Karna, P.M. Chacko, C.L. Imchen, Nikhlesh Kumar, Dr. I.L. Aier and Dr. A.K. Nonkynrih for their valuable encouragement and academic inspiration during the course of my research at the Department of Sociology, NEHU.

My thanks to the research helper in each ward (Kohima) and all the respondents for their kind co-operation during the course of my fieldwork.

I am grateful to ICSSR North Eastern Regional Centre, Shillong and its Director, Dr C Joshua Thomas for his encouragement and also for the contingency grant which the Centre provided to me during the course of my research work. I appreciate much the secretarial assistance extended by Ms Christine Blah of the ICSSR-NERC.

Mr. M.P. Misra of Akansha Publishing House, New Delhi deserves special thanks for agreeing to bring out my research work in this book format.

Lastly I am much indebted to my parents and my dear wife Naro for their support all through the study.

Kohima
May, 2006

KEDILEZO KIKHI

Contents

LIST OF TABLES

1

Introduction

This chapter introduces the problem of the study, attempts to study unemployment and highlights the various kinds of unemployment. Educated unemployment has been discussed and the age bracket for the youth is focused. The universe of the study, the objectives and the methodology - sampling frame adopted has also been discussed in this chapter.

I. THE PROBLEM OF THE STUDY:

Nagaland is a state having a weak industrial sector and an underdeveloped agriculture, bulk of the educated population being dependent on the service-sector. We can see that the educational institutions in Nagaland are continuously producing educated youths but employment opportunities are limited in relation to supply of labour. There is no balance between the supply of workers and the demand for their services. Thus, open unemployment occurs because able and willing educated persons are in search of work, but there is no work for them and they remain unemployed.

The problem is menacing because: i) These intelligent people, can become dangerously vocal and influential not to accept any unenviable position lying down and can give constant threat to the security and stability of the state. ii) It is a waste for educated people to remain idle for they constitute the best of our human resources, valuable human capital (Puttaswamaiah, 1977).

Atchly (1977) believes that the greatest tragedy for a woman is widowhood and for a man unemployment (joblessness).

A man has to perform many roles in his life, the most crucial of which is to be an earning member. It is crucial not because a man spends approximately one-third of his lifetime performing this role but because it determines both his livelihood and status. It also enables an individual to support his family and fulfill his social obligations to the society. It makes possible for him to achieve power too. If a person having capacity and potential to work, refuses to work or fails to obtain work, he not only loses respect or status in the society but also becomes an emotional and social liability. (Ahuja, 1997). It has been rightly observed that: "Unemployment is a great evil, it is a poison, and it pollutes the society and wrecks the political fibre of a country. It creates devils, it turns good man into bad, and it changes an honest worker into a criminal. It encourages dishonesty, patronizes corruption, glorifies falsehood, points out the dark side of human character and makes one blind to its good side. It is difficult to expect truth; nobility and honesty from a person who cannot have two square meals a day, and cannot provide a morsel of food or a dose of medicine to his sick wife or ailing children. A half-clad and half-fed man is a diseased man and a diseased man infects the nation, the fire of hunger consumes all the noble virtues of a father, duties of a son or a husband." (Mamoria, 1954).

Even though considerable studies have been done on the Naga society, the problem of educated unemployment remains a neglected topic of study, though it is one of the first rate state problem. This study is an attempt to answer a number of sociological questions like - the socio-economic background of educated unemployed youth; their aspirations, preferences and expectations; the multi-social problems of unemployed youth; and its related social consequences.

II. A) UNEMPLOYMENT:

Many, especially by Economist and others from time to time, have defined the concept of unemployment. But, only a few of these academic definitions by social scientists are taken as a working definition for our study purpose. Unemployment is admittedly the most significant and perplexing of all labour problems, and today it has become a universal problem. The unemployment problem in our country should be viewed not as a 'residual' problem to be tackled after the other problems have been solved, but as a 'primary' problem. Economists have explained unemployment in terms of lack of capital, lack of investment, and high production. Some believe that unemployment has its roots in the decline of the business cycle following a period of industrial prosperity. A few hold that dislocations in the industries and an inability to forecast the market have put a sizeable proportion of men out of work. Yet others are of the opinion that sudden economic deflation and impersonal forces of economic competition cause loss of work. Improvements in machine technology, over production, falsely stimulated speculation, social emphasis upon monetary success and the inevitable depressions - all these make for crippling disruption in the demand of labour.

Mali (1989) in his book "*Economic Problems and Planning in Assam*" states that rapid growth of population; slow industrial growth; traditional agricultural practice; poor growth of economy; increase in educational facilities; immobility of labour force; attitude of the people; are the main causes of unemployment.

According to *Raj Krishna*, there are four major criterias by which a person may be called unemployed (1973).

i) The first is the *time criterion* - by which a person may be called unemployed or under-employed if he is gainfully occupied during the year for a number of hours or days less than some normal hours or days defined as full employment hours or days.

ii) The second is the *income criterion* - according to which a person is considered to be unemployed if he earns an income per year less than some desirable minimum. This can be termed as the poverty criterion of unemployment because the person has secured some work but the income for the work is less than the acceptable minimum.

iii) The third criterion is the *willingness criterion*. A person may be called under-employed if he is willing to do more than he is doing at present. Such a person may either be actively searching for more work or be available for more if it is referred to him on terms to which he is accustomed.

A person may find that the income from the work that he is currently doing is less than what he considers to be an adequate minimum income and, therefore, he may be actively searching for more work.

iv) The fourth criterion is the *productivity criterion*. According to this criterion, a person may be called unemployed or under-employed if he is removable from his present employment and this factor would not reduce the total output. This is the case of 'disguised unemployment'.

The *National Sample Survey Organisation* has classified employed and unemployed persons with the following approaches:

i) *Usual status approach*: According to this approach, a person engaged in gainful work for more than half the days in a reference year is a 'usual principal status' worker and which is likely to continue in the future. A person who pursues some gainful work for less than half of the 365 days is a 'usual subsidiary status' worker. Persons belonging to these two categories constitute the category of the employed. On the other hand a person is not working but is looking or available for work for more than half of the days in the year, is unemployed. And if a person who is neither working nor seeking nor available for more than half of the year is not in 'labour force'.

ii) *Current weekly status approach*: According to this approach, a person who is engaged in any gainful activity for at least one hour on any day of the reference week is employed. And a person who does not work for even one hour on any day but is seeking or is available for work at a time during the week is considered available for work (or unemployed). Others are considered 'not available' for work (or not in labour force).

iii) *Current daily status approach*: Under this approach, a person engaged in any gainful activity for four hours or more during the reference day is employed for the whole day. And, a person who works for one hour or more but less than four hours is considered employed for the half day. If a person who does not work but is seeking or available for work more than or less than four hours a day is unemployed for the whole day or half day respectively.

P.C. Mahalanobis has observed three possibilities regarding the measurement of unemployment and under-employment (1985):

i) Those who have jobs carrying daily or monthly wages or salaries are, employed; and those who have jobs of this type, but has lost them or are seeking such jobs are unemployed.

ii) Another possibility is to think in terms of a hypothetical normal output per unit of time (hour, day, week, month, etc.) and ascertain whether a person is termed out of the full amount or only a fraction of it.

iii) Thirdly, there is the approach of thinking in terms of normal earnings and enquiring whether a person is earning the full amount or only a fraction of it.

In 1954, the *International Conference of Labour Statistician* adopted the standard international definition of unemployed as:

1) Persons in unemployment consists of all persons above a specific age who, on the specified day or for a specified week, are in the following categories:

    a) Workers available for employment whose contract of employment has been terminated or temporarily suspended and who is without a job and seeking work for pay or profit.

    b) Persons who are available for work (except for minor illness) during the specified period and are seeking work for pay or profit, who are never previously employed or whose most recent status is other than that of an employee, i.e., former employers etc. or who has been in retirement.

    c) Persons on temporary or indefinite lay-off without pay.

2) The following categories of persons are not considered to be unemployed:

a) Persons intending to establish their own business or farm, but who have not yet arranged to do so, and not seeking work for pay or profit.

b) Former unpaid family workers not at work and not seeking work.

In short, this definition demands of those to be categorized as unemployed that they be i) 'not working' and ii) 'seeking work', a combination which is particularly difficult to sustain in a developing economy like India.

Different purposes call for different definitions. Further the definitions that are implicit in the official figures published in different countries vary because of the way in which unemployed statistics are compiled. It is not an equally clear-cut conception. Technical definition as supplied by various governments in reply to an *International Labour Office* questionnaire (1934) is as follows:

1) *Belgium*: Unemployment is a lack of work which affects a person who is normally engaged as a wage-earner or salaried employee and which is due to some cause independent of his own will other than any physical incapacity.

   a) 'Total unemployment' is unemployment affecting a worker whose contract of service has been terminated by the employer and has given evidence of his intention to find other employee.

   b) 'Intermittent unemployment' is unemployment affecting a worker whose contract of service has not been terminated but in whose case the normal quantity of service rendered, and consequently the earnings, have been reduced owing to lack of work.

2) *Great Britain*: A person is unemployed on any day -

   a) On which he does not work under a contract of service.

   b) In respect of which he is not entitled to wages under a contract of service.

   c) On which he is not following any occupation from which he derives remuneration or profit; and

   d) Which is not a holiday at the establishment where he works.

3) *Italy*: Total unemployment is the state of inactivity suffered by a worker in spite of his intention to find work and in spite of his physical fitness to carry on his trade or calling. Partial unemployment is the state in which a worker finds himself when, owing to causes independent of his own will and his physical fitness, he gives his services for less than half the time which is recognized in the labour market as the normal for the particular kind of unemployment.

4) *Switzerland*: All persons who habitually exercise a regular occupation for remuneration, who are willing to work, who are suitable for employment, and who, for the time being, are unable to earn their usual remuneration for no fault of their own, shall be deemed to be unemployed.

5) *Yugoslavia*: Unemployment means a total or partial lack of work suffered by a worker either involuntary or voluntary but for good reason:

   a) Total unemployment means a lack of work resulting in the complete loss of the only economy resources available to provide the minimum needs of livelihood.

   b) Partial unemployment means a lack of work resulting in a partial loss of the only economic resources available to provide the minimum needs of livelihood.

From these ad hoc' definitions of unemployment some general notion of what constitutes unemployment may be drawn.

Dholakia states unemployment as a state of being without gainful work and generally considers it as an involuntary failure to get income yielding work (1977). *Thakur* defines that when an individual even after his best possible efforts, does not get work on the existing wage rate or even at low wage rate to earn his means of subsistence, he is termed as 'unemployed' as well as 'poor' (1985). *Sinclair* has stressed the need to define unemployment negatively by stipulating what it is not, i.e. unemployment is clearly not employment and so the unemployed are a subset of those who are not employed (1987).

A society is believed to be in a "condition of full employment" if the period enforced idleness remains minimum. A society with full employment has four characteristics:

a) An individual takes very little time to find remunerative work according to his capabilities and qualifications.

b) He is sure of finding remunerative work.

c) The number of vacant jobs in the society exceeds the number of job seekers and,

d) Work is available on 'adequate remuneration' (Ahuja, 1997).

D'Mello has defined unemployment as a "condition in which an individual is not in a state of remunerative occupation despite his desire to do so" (1969). *Naba* has explained unemployment as a "condition of involuntary idleness" (1968). *The Planning Commission of India* has described a person as 'marginally unemployed' when he/she remains without work for 6 months a year. *Bajpai* refers unemployment to the condition of joblessness in one's life (1992).

Unemployment refers to a situation where persons who are able to work and also willing to work at the prevailing rate of wages, does not find work. This is an involuntary idleness leading to wastage of labour. It is not confined to any category of persons. It may be among the unskilled, high skilled and technically qualified persons. Able-bodied persons who voluntarily remain unemployed are excluded from the concept of unemployment.

An unemployed person therefore, is - one having potentialities and willingness to earn, but is unable to find a remunerative work. It has three elements:

i) An individual should be capable of working.

ii) An individual should be willing to work.

iii) An individual must make an effort to find work.

B) YOUTH:

Youth has been defined as the early part of life especially the period between childhood and adult age; and the youth population constitutes a significant segment in any given society. When we talk of youth as a stage in human development, obviously "there is a biological process which sets in at birth (or more precisely at conception) and continues until the individual reaches maturity in terms of the species" (Berger, 1972). *Friedman* has defined youth as "the group of human beings who have reached the end puberty but have not yet acquired the full rights and duties of adult life" (1971). In modern societies, the period between childhood and adulthood has been lengthened due to prolonged education and preparation for the future. Due to expanding education including college education, vocational and professional education - it has made the roles of a young person more important and for longer periods. On recognizing the importance of youth in the wake of the rapid economic development, urbanization and changing life style in today's world, the United Nations designated the year 1985 as the International Youth Year with the theme 'Participation, Development and Peace'. The WHO observes that today's youth stands at the point of transition, not only in its sojourn from childhood to adulthood, but also stands at the threshold between traditional and modern ways of life.

In order to launch any meaningful policy and programme for the youth, it is essential to determine the age bracket that constitutes youth. But it is difficult to accurately assign lower and upper age limits for the youth. Because, this vary from time to time, and also from society to society. The time span required for biological maturation differs from person to person. To *Kuppuswamy*, early youth would refer to the 13 to 19 years age group (1984). To some others, it refers to the 12 to early 30's (Chauhan, 1990). The UNO has categorized youth to be between the age group of 15-24 years.

In India, for census operations, and in accordance with the practice of the government of India, the age group of 15-34 is recognized as youth; which is further classified into three groups: i) 15-19 years as sub-junior, ii) 20-24 years as junior, iii) 25-34 years as senior youth (Saraswathi, 1988). Accordingly, the youth age bracket for the purpose of this study is taken between 15-34 years.

C) EDUCATED:

All those who have completed at least eleven years of schooling and are matriculate and above are considered to be educated (Ahamad, 1973).

The comprehensive working definition of an 'educated unemployed youth' for the present study is therefore identified as - anyone between the age group of 15 - 34 years from matriculate to the post graduate level, who is capable of working, willing to work and making an effort to find work but is unable to find any remunerative job.

III. KINDS OF UNEMPLOYMENT:

It is extremely useful to be able to distinguish various kinds of unemployment. In the classification that have been attempted, the categories that one most frequently encounters bear the titles 'frictional', 'seasonal', 'cyclical', (or 'deficiency- of-demand') and 'structural' unemployment. *Ahuja* (1997) has classified unemployment either as rural or urban, or as seasonal, cyclical and technological. Urban unemployment has been sub-classified as educational and industrial. *Puttaswamaiah* (1977) has classified unemployment as i) voluntary and ii) involuntary. Again, involuntary has been sub-classified as disguised, visible and seasonal.

1) Frictional and seasonal unemployment

When there is a minimum 'float' of workers in the process of moving to new jobs - it is termed as 'minimum frictional unemployment'. Seasonal unemployment is frequently included in this notion of frictional unemployment. It is perhaps the oldest concept of all. Some industries or occupation are seasonal in character such as ice-cream factories and boatmen's services in the UK, which have peak demand during the summer. Also as in India, agriculture could be safely recorded under this head.

2) Cyclical unemployment

'Cyclical' unemployment frequently termed 'deficiency-of-demand' is that the total demand for goods and services, given existent wage rates and labour productivity, is not sufficient to generate jobs for all those who want to work. The number of job vacancies open in the economy as a whole is significantly less than the total number of people seeking work.

3) *Structural unemployment*:

It implies:

a) There are particular sectors of the labour force from which workers cannot easily and quickly move into other sectors in search of jobs.

b) In some or all of these sectors with impaired mobility, unemployment significantly exceeds available vacancies. And because of inadequate mobility, labour supply does not easily adjust to the inadequate level of demand.

c) Insufficient demand for particular types of labour for a number of reasons:

   i) First, the demand for particular skills may be reduced because of technological change or a shift in the pattern of demand.

   ii) Secondly, there may be a shift of economic activity out of a geographical region not matched by a comparable exodus of workers. This leads to the problem of depressed areas.

   iii) And third, there may be an influx of workers - of a particular type or into, a particular region - at such a rate that they cannot be quickly absorbed into jobs.

4) Technological unemployment:

It is a situation when the given output catering for a constant level of demand is produced by lesser number of workers owing to the adoption of improved technologies; and consequently, the present surplus workers become unemployed.

IV. EDUCATED UNEMPLOYMENT:

Educated unemployment refers to the unemployment not only of graduates but also of all those who have completed at least eleven years of schooling and are matriculate and above. The educated unemployed is a dangerous person. The unemployed persons belonging to this category are not 'dumb, driven cattle'. He nurses a sense of personal injury and if the grievances are long continued and the numbers involved are large, the situation can be decidedly explosive too. The most important aspect of this problem is the rapidly increasing unemployment amongst the educated youth year after year.

In India, even after 45 years of socio-economic planning, the problem of unemployment in general and of the educated persons in particular has remained critical and defied of an early solution, although in every successive five year plan, huge investments have been made and job creation has remained one of the objective (Q.U.Khan, 1996). Again, the data on the census, Live Register, suffer from a number of limitations. The problem with the census data is that, for those not working, they do not make any distinction between those who are seeking or available for work and those who are not i.e., i) the unemployed and ii) those out of the work force. The limitation of the employment exchange data is that: i) all the unemployed persons are not registered with the exchanges and ii) also not all of those who are registered are actually unemployed.

The Directorate General of Employment and Training (DGE&T) found out that about half of the persons registered as unemployed are not really unemployed. It has published the results of the survey in 1991 - actually unemployed as given in Table 1.1 below:

Table 1.1
Actually Unemployed (DGE&T)

1.	Illiterate	51.7 %
2.	Literate but below matric	56.2 %
3.	Matriculates	55.4 %
4.	Under-graduates	56.5 %
5.	Graduates and above	57.7 %
	All	55.3 %

Source: Survey, 1991.

The problem of educated unemployment has increased from time to time in spite of various opportunities for the educated unemployed. And the reasons that has caused this increased trend are many. Some important reasons relating to India could be:

i) Over production of the educated.

ii) Uncontrolled expansion of secondary and higher education.

iii) Wrong kind of education: the system of education is highly related to life. In fact, one of the University Grants Commission (UGC) annual reports stated clearly that the present system of education is generating much waste and stagnation. The Kothari Commission (1964-66) also admitted that there is a wide gulf between the contents of national development (Ahuja, 1997).

iv) The educated persons prefer white-collar to manual and industrial jobs.

v) The secondary and higher education has been adopting the policy of 'invite-all' or 'open-door' generating maximum number of educated unemployment.

As such the rate of unemployment in India among the educated youth has manifested increasing proportions during 1965-77; the number of unemployment graduates rose at the rate of 21% annually (from 9 lakh in 1965 to 5.6 million in 1977). Then, during 1980-88, their number rose at the rate of 23% every year, and between Jan. 1988 and Jan. 1989, the percentage increased by 19.2. The educated job seekers (matriculation and above) constitute over 60% of the registered unemployed. According to the Planning Commission, the number of educated unemployed in our country in 1992 is 7 million. Since about 3 million youth enter the labour market every year, 16 to 17 million unemployed youth are expected to be added to the existing 7 million by 1998 or the total number of unemployed youth by the end of 1998 will be 23 to 24 million. Of these 14 million educated youth are expected to have got jobs between 1992 and 1997, which will have between 7 and 8 million educated youth unemployed by the end of 1997 (The Hindustan Times, Sept.15, 1996). The problem of unemployment among the educated is a major area of concern. Table 1.2 below gives the estimates of unemployment rate among the educated and their share in the total unemployed.

While the incidence of unemployment among the educated has shown a decreasing trend over the period, 1977-78 to 1993-94, the share of the educated among the unemployed has risen during this period. The incidence of unemployment among the educated is very high. In 1993-94, it is 9.6% as against the overall unemployment rate of 1.9% on usual status basis.

Table 1.2
Unemployment rate (usual status) among the Educated (Secondary Education Plus) Youth (age 15 plus).

Year	Unemployment Rate	Percent share of educated in Total Unemployed
1977-78	15.4	28.8
1983	11.3	43.7
1987-88	11.8	39.9
1993-94	9.6	62.0

(*The Indian Journal of Labour Economics*, Jan-March, 1999).

In Nagaland, there has been an alarming rise of educated unemployed youth (matric and above) adversely affecting them. The total number of unemployed, which was 22,069 in 1991 on the live register, had risen to 37,090 in 2000, which is a percentage increase of 68.06%. The state had 10,534 registered educated unemployed in 1991, whereas the figure rose to 22,119 in 2000. The Kohima District alone had 12,690 educated unemployed persons by 2000 on the live register.

Over the period from 1991 to 2000, we could see the increasing share of educated unemployed youth as against the overall unemployment i.e., the total registered job seekers. The educated unemployed youth, which constitutes 42.73% of total unemployed in 1991, has risen to 70.30% in 1998, 60.84% in 1999, and to 59.64 in 2000. Today the state is also experiencing the rapid expansion of education, and the educated youth has become its worst victim.

V. UNIVERSE OF STUDY:

Different scholars in the country have conducted various studies of unemployment from time to time. But so far, no one has attempted to go for such a study in the state, though it has become the first rate state problem. The universe of the study is Kohima Town in particular and Nagaland at large, as a backdrop. Kohima, being the capital town of Nagaland has an influx of people, particularly youth from all parts of the state - for education and employment. Thus the territorial representation of the study is exclusive and fairly representative.

At the time of study, Kohima Town has the following 15 wards under its civic jurisdiction:

i) Ward no.01: a) High School Colony, b) Bayavü Hill, c) Sepfüzou.

ii) Ward no.02: a) Kenuozou, b) Kezieke, c) N.P.S.Area, d) Mission Compound, e) Veterinary Colony, f) Gourilane.

iii) Ward no.03: a) Nagabazar.

iv) Ward no.04: a) Chotobosti.

v) Ward no.05: a) D.Block.

vi) Ward no.06: a) Daklane, b) C.Block (Part I).

vii) Ward no.07: a) New Market, b) C.Block (Part II).

viii) Ward no.08: a) Midlane.

ix) Ward no.09: a) Hospital Colony, b) Officer's Hill.

x) Ward no.10: a) P.W.D. Colony.

xi) Ward no.11: a) Chandmari.

xii) Ward no.12: a) Poterlane, b) Old Minister's Hill.

xiii) Ward no.13: a) A.G. Colony, b) New Minister's Hill, c) Lirie, d) N.S.T.Colony.

xiv) Ward no.14: a) P.R. Hill, b) Supply Point, c) Jail Colony.

xv) Ward no.15: a) Agri. Colony, b) Forest Colony, c) Para Medical Colony.

VI. OBJECTIVES OF STUDY:

The research study is conducted with the following aims and objectives:

a) To study in Kohima Town - the magnitude and trend of educated unemployment and employment opportunities for educated youth.

b) To examine the social and educational background of educated unemployed youth.

c) To explore the aspirations, nature and kind of job preferred by the unemployed.

d) To highlight the problems and find the social consequences of educated unemployed youth, and

e) To examine various governmental measures, policies for educated unemployed youth.

VII. METHOD OF STUDY:

Since the study is conducted to explore, examine and analyze - to understand the problems of educated unemployed youth, the approach throughout the study has been analytical and evaluative.

The study has been focused upon educated unemployed youth of 15-34 years of age, from the post-matric to the post-graduate level. This has been respectively broken into i) matric; ii) pre-university/class xii covering arts, science and the commerce streams; iii) graduates covering the general streams or the so called 'literary' faculties: arts, science, commerce and law, and the non-general streams or the technical or the so called practical' faculties: engineering and medicine; iv) post-graduate level covering the general streams: arts, science, commerce and law, and the non-general streams: engineering and medicine. And thus, the sample is sorted out by purposively selected sampling technique of 240 respondents of 16 each i.e., as broken up above: matric = 1, pre-university = 3 (1 each from the streams of arts, science, commerce), graduates = 6 (1each from the streams of arts, science, commerce, law and 1 each from engineering, medicine), post-graduates = 6 (1 each from arts, science, commerce, law and 1 each from engineering, medicine); from the 15 wards/sectors that constitutes the urban area of the town under the civic jurisdiction of the Kohima Town Committee. This sampling is purposively selected on the basis of different faculty and on the basis of different educational qualification, for the needful study but some streams like management, agriculture, education, computers etc. have been omitted because of their negligible presence.

For data collection, both primary and secondary sources are used - with primary data as the main emphasis. A questionnaire, which consists of 128 questions, is the main research tool for collection of the primary data. The questionnaire is divided into 6 sections, consisting of 104 close-ended questionnaires and 24 open-ended questionnaires. The collection of secondary data is from the reviews of relevant literature, journals and magazines, newspapers, research and survey conducted by various organizations viz: the Census Reports, the National Sample Surveys (NSS), the Directorate General of Employment and Training (DGE&T), Dissertations, the Directorate of Employment and Craftsmen Training, the Employment Exchanges, the Directorate of Economics and Statistics, the Annual Administrative Reports etc.

VIII. SAMPLING FRAME:

Keeping in view the two limitations of the Employment Exchanges i.e.

i) All the unemployed persons are not registered with exchanges ii) also not all of those who are registered are actually unemployed; and the various short comings mentioned in relevant literatures; a brief pilot survey is conducted - to find out how many educated unemployed youth in Kohima have not registered in the Employment Exchange. Therefore, the researcher did not select the respondents based on any Employment Exchanges. But the respondents are disproportionately and randomly selected on academic discipline and educational qualification basis - in order to facilitate the research work for better analysis, proper diagnosis, and fair treatment with all categories of educated unemployed youth. It is a precaution to keep the study free from any bias or prejudice ensuring a fair, representative and balance sample.

For better efficiency and faster progress of the work, the researcher has kept a helper in each ward who is to assist him. The helper is also one of the respondents in his/her respective ward. The researcher with the assistance of the helper has to work hard to locate the respondents, make them understand the importance and purpose of study, essentiality of their sincere response - which is the toughest. The respondents are also assured that their response will be used only for research purpose and kept confidential. And then, with the help of the helper in each respective ward, the questionnaires are distributed and collected one by one. It took 8 months for the researcher to complete all the 15 wards in Kohima Town.

As shown in Table 1.3, out of 240 total respondents, only 193 respondents could be available and distributed with questionnaires whereas the remaining 47 respondents could not be available with the required qualification in their respective wards. Those unavailable respondents in their respective wards are: B.E = 1 (in ward no. 14); M.B.B.S = 4 (in ward nos. 05, 07, 11, 13); L.L.B = 3 (in ward nos. 05, 07, 12); M.A = 1 (in ward no.11); M.SC = 1 (in ward no. 12); M.Com = 4 (in ward nos. 03, 06, 10, 11); M.E = 13 (in ward nos. 01, 02, 03, 04, 05, 06, 07, 08, 09, 10, 11, 13, 14); M.D = 12 (inward nos. 01, 02, 03, 04, 05, 06, 07, 08, 09, 11, 12, 15); L.L.M = 8 (in ward nos. 02, 04, 06, 08, 09, 10, 11, 12). (It has to be noted that the educated youth having the required qualifications are already employed which falls outside the study). Again, in 193 available respondents, 2 respondents i.e. 1 PU. (Sc) in ward no.15 and 1 B.SC in ward no. 08 could not give back the questionnaires.

As shown in Table 1.3, 191 respondents (completely filled in questionnaires) constituted about 79.58% against the total 240 respondents. This respondent's chart / % of respondent's representation can be further studied as shown in the Table on two bases: (a) educational qualification and (b) ward basis.

Accordingly on (a) *educational qualification basis*, the representation is:

i) **Matriculate:** total respondents = 15, respondents % against the total = 7.85, and respondents response rate = 100.00.

ii) **Pre-university:** total respondents = 44, respondents % against the total = 23.04, and respondents response rate = 97.78.

iii) **Graduate:** total respondents = 81, respondents % against the total = 42.41, and respondents response rate = 90.00.

iv) **Post-graduate:** total respondents = 51, respondents % against the total = 26.70, and respondents response rate = 56.67.

(b) *On ward basis*, the representation is:

i) Ward no. 01: total respondents = 14, respondents response rate = 93.33, and respondents % against the total = 7.33.

ii) Ward no. 02: total respondents = 13, respondents response rate = 86.67, and respondents % against the total = 6.81.

iii) Ward no. 03: total respondents = 14, respondents response rate = 93.33, and respondents % against the total = 7.33.

iv) Ward no. 04: total respondents = 12, respondents response rate = 80.00, and respondents % against the total = 6.28.

v) Ward no. 05: total respondents = 12, respondents response rate = 80.00, and respondents % against the total = 6.28.

vi) Ward no. 06: total respondents = 12, respondents response rate = 80.00, and respondents % against the total = 6.28.

vii) Ward no. 07: total respondents = 12, respondents response rate = 80.00, and respondents % against the total = 6.28.

viii) Ward no. 08: total respondents = 12, respondents response rate = 80.00, and respondents % against the total = 6.28.

ix) Ward no. 09: total respondents = 13, respondents response rate = 86.67, and respondents % against the total = 6.81.

x) Ward no. 10: total respondents = 13, respondents response rate = 86.67, and respondents % against the total = 6.81.

xi) Ward no. 11: total respondents = 10, respondents response rate = 66.67, and respondents % against the total = 5.24.

xii) Ward no. 12: total respondents = 12, respondents response rate = 80.00, and respondents % against the total = 6.28.

xiii) Ward no. 13: total respondents = 14, respondents response rate = 93.33, and respondents % against the total = 7.33.

Table 1.3: Respondent Chart / % of Respondent Representation Educational Qualification/Ward Basis.

(Respondent-each ward = 16 i.e. matriculate = 1,
pre-university (10+2) = 3, graduate = 6, post-graduate = 6).
(Total Respondent for 15 wards = 15 × 16 = 240).

Sl No.	Ward/Colony	Education Qualification																Total	R. Res-ponse Rate	R. % against the Total
		Matric	Pre-University 10+2			Graduate						Post Graduate								
			A	Sc	C	A	Sc	C	E	M	L	A	Sc	C	E	M	L			
01	**Ward No. 01**																			
(i)	High School Colony																			
(ii)	Bayavu Hill																			
(iii)	Sepfuzu	1	1	1	1	1	1	1	1	1	1	1	1	1	-	-	1	14	93.33	7.33
02	**Ward No. 02**																			
(i)	Kenuozou																			
(ii)	Kezieke																			
(iii)	N.P.S. Area																			

(iv) Mission Compound																			
(v) Vet. Colony																			
(vi) Gourilane	1	1	1	1	1	1	1	1	1	1	1	1	1	-	-	-	13	86.67	6.81
03 Ward No. 03																			
(i) Nagabazar	1	1	1	1	1	1	1	1	1	1	1	1	1	-	-	1	14	93.33	7.33
04 Ward No. 04																			
(i) Chotobosti	1	1	1	1	1	1	1	1	1	1	1	1	-	-	-	-	12	80.00	6.28
05 Ward No. 05																			
(i) D. Block	1	1	1	1	1	1	1	1	-	-	1	1	1	-	-	1	12	80.00	6.28
06 Ward No. 06																			
(i) Daklane																			
(ii) C. Block (Part I)	1	1	1	1	1	1	1	1	1	1	1	1	-	-	-	-	12	80.00	6.28
07 Ward No. 07																			
(i) New Market																			
(ii) C. Block (Part II)	1	1	1	1	1	1	1	1	-	-	1	1	1	-	-	1	12	80.00	6.28
08 Ward No. 08																			
(i) Midlane	1	1	1	1	1	-	1	1	1	1	1	1	1	-	-	-	12	80.00	6.28

(Contd.)

Table 1.3 (Contd.)

Sl No.	Ward/Colony	Matric	Pre-University 10+2			Graduate						Post Graduate						Total	R. Response Rate	R. % against the Total
			A	Sc	C	A	Sc	C	E	M	L	A	Sc	C	E	M	L			
09	**Ward No. 09**																			
(i)	Hospital Colony																			
(ii)	Officer's Hill	1	1	1	1	1	1	1	1	1	1	1	1	1	-	-	-	13	86.67	6.81
10	**Ward No. 10**																			
(i)	P.W.D. Colony	1	1	1	1	1	1	1	1	1	1	1	1	-	-	1	-	13	86.67	6.81
11	**Ward No. 11**																			
(i)	Chandmari	1	1	1	1	1	1	1	1	-	1	-	1	-	-	-	-	10	66.67	5.24
12	**Ward No. 12**																			
(i)	Porterlane																			
(ii)	Old Ministers' Hill	1	1	1	1	1	1	1	1	1	-	1	-	1	1	-	-	12	80.00	6.28
13	**Ward No. 13**																			
(i)	A.G. Colony																			

(ii) New Minister' Hills																			
(iii) Lirie																			
(iv) N.S.T. Colony	1	1	1	1	1	1	1	1	-	1	1	1	1	-	1	1	14	93.33	7.33
14 Ward No. 14																			
(i) P.R. Hill																			
(ii) Supply Point																			
(iii) Jail Colony	1	1	1	1	1	1	.1	-	1	1	1	1	1	-	1	1	14	93.33	7.33
15 Ward No. 15																			
(i) Agri Colony																			
(ii) Forest Colony																			
(iii) Para Medical Colony	1	1	-	1	1	1	1	1	1	1	1	1	1	1	-	1	14	93.33	7.33
Total	15	44					81						51				191		
Respondent's % against the total	7.85	23.04					42.41						26.70				100.00		
Respondent's Response Rate	100	97.78					90.00						56.67				79.58		

(A = arts, Sc = science, C = commerce, E = engineering, M = medicine, L = law), (R = Respondent).

xiv) Ward no. 14: total respondents = 14, respondents response rate = 93.33, and respondents % against the total = 7.33.

xv) Ward no. 15: total respondents = 14, respondents response rate = 93.33, and respondents % against the total = 7.33.

As given in the Tables below, it is found that, 54.97 percent of educated unemployed youth have registered in Employment Exchanges, while 45.03 percent have not registered. The sample contains 36.65 percent female, and 63.35 percent male educated unemployed youth. The mean age of the respondents is found to be 24.51 years, and mode period to be 25 - 29 years. The sample has 95.81 percent Christians, 3.14 percent Hindus, no Muslims and 1.05 percent others like Pagans etc. The sample also has 6.81 percent married persons, 92.67 percent unmarried and 0.52 percent divorcees. The sample has 71.73 respondents with nuclear family backgrounds, 14.66 percent from joint families, 10.47 percent from extended family and 3.14 percent from divorced families.

Table 1.4

Distribution of sample by qualification/faculty

Matriculate	15
PU	15
PU (Sc)	14
PU (Com)	15
BA	15
B.Sc	14
B.Com	15
BE	14
MBBS	11
LLB	12
MA	14
M.Sc	14
M.Com	11
M.E	02
M.D.	03
LLM	07
Total	191

Table 1.5
Distribution of Sample by Registration

Registered	**105 (54.97)**
Not Registered	86 (45.03)

Table 1.6
Distribution of sample by sex

Male	**121 (63.35)**
Female	70 (36.65)

Table 1.7
Distribution of sample by age

15 - 19	18 (9.43)
20 - 24	68 (35.60)
25 - 29	**96 (50.26)**
30 - 34	09 (4.71)
Mode Period	25 - 29
Mean	24.51

Table 1.8
Distribution of sample by marital status

Married	13 (6.81)
Unmarried	**177 (92.67)**
Divorced family	01 (0.52)
Widow/widower	00

Table 1.9
Distribution of sample by religion

Christianity	**183 (95.81)**
Hindu	06 (3.14)
Muslim	00
Others	02 (1.05)

Table 1.10
Distribution of sample by type of family

Nuclear	**137 (71.73)**
Joint	28 (14.66)
Extended	20 (10.47)
Divorced family	06 (3.14)

2

Unemployment - Magnitude and Trend

This chapter attempts to work out the broad magnitude and trend of educated unemployment in Nagaland as revealed by the Employment Exchange statistics. The study focuses on ten-year period (decade) from 1991 to 2000. It reveals the increased percentages of job seekers on the Live Register, the yearly expansion of unemployment in the state, the high proportion of educated unemployed against the total unemployed, the probability of an unemployed person to get a job, and the sex-wise distributed proportion of educated unemployed youth. This chapter also makes an intensive study on the sharp trend of educated unemployment in the capital district, i.e. Kohima.

It is necessary to analyze the magnitude and trend of unemployed youth for three reasons:

i) firstly, the bulk of the total unemployed at most times does not get highlighted as it should be.

ii) Secondly, with the increase in the literacy rate, unemployment among the educated youth is described to be 'twice cursed' for the economy since education is highly subsidized in the country. The state expenditure on building this human capital goes to waste.

iii) The third reason for analyzing youth unemployment is to highlight the social and political ramifications of idle youth.

> Elementary empirical evidence suggests that the states/ regions having high unemployment rates among youth have given rise to militancy, crime, and separatist movements as they are easy prey for disruptive elements in society (Aggarwal and Goyal, 2000).

The nature of unemployment differs and the causes vary from developed to developing economies. In developed economies of the West, effective demand is directly correlated to unemployment. Rise in effective demand leads to rise in employment and fall in effective demand leads to a fall in employment. However in under-developed economies like India, unemployment is generally structural.

In the state of Nagaland, with no proper industrial sector, under-developed agriculture, and only small size of the service sector - employment opportunities are limited in relation to supply of labour. Open unemployment occurs because able and willing persons are in search of work, but there is no work for them and they remain unemployed. This is clearly reflected by the number of persons registered with the Employment Exchanges. The severity of the kinds of unemployment, however, varies from state to state in the country.

I. MAGNITUDE AND TREND - NAGALAND:

It is to be noted that adequate and reliable data for estimating the unemployment figure in Nagaland is difficult to get. However, this study is a serious attempt to study about the unemployment situation in the state, based upon the number of job seekers registered with the Employment Exchange Centres. The Employment Exchange data, however, has limitations: i.e. i) the data mainly covers urban areas only ii) large numbers of the unemployed does not get themselves registered with these Centres for the reason that they are not effective and iii) also not all of those who are registered are actually unemployed. The unemployed youth from the rural areas are not properly covered and thus, leaving a large number of unemployed outside the arena. Again many youth from the villages are not even aware that such Exchange exists. Those unemployed who does not register saying the Exchanges are not effective, seems to be convinced that they are never getting job through the

Employment Exchange. In addition, many are least bothered to renew their registration. There are some among those registered who will keep on maintaining their registration by renewing until they get a satisfactory job. Hence, a study of unemployment from the Employment Exchange data will provide only a partial picture of the problem in the state. However, in the absence of any other dependable sources of information, we have to rely on this.

As shown in Table 2.1, a summary of the important statistics of Employment Exchanges in Nagaland as on 31st December 2000 is: 01 Regional Employment Exchange, 06 District Employment Exchange, 02 Rural Employment Bureau, 01 Coaching-Cum-Guidance Centre, 02 Industrial Training Institute, 01 Women Industrial Training Institute, 01 Self-Employment Promotion Cell, and 01 Physically Handicapped Cell. All this offices are being operating since many years but its effectiveness to help through the youth has become a big question. Like for example, The Industrial Training Institute gives training to many youth at different intervals, but there is no guarantee for these trained youth to get a job. Or these trained youth do not take up self-employed jobs as they are expected, which either is due to lack of sufficient fund or improper training, lack of interests, etc.

Table 2.1

Summary of the important statistics of Employment Exchanges in Nagaland as on 31st December 2000.

1	Regional Employment Exchange	01
2	District Employment Exchange	06
3	Rural Employment Bureau	02
4	Coaching-Cum-Guidance Centre	01
5	Industrial Training Institute	02
6	Women Industrial Training Institute	01
7	Self-Employment Promotion Cell	01
8	Physically Handicapped Cell	01
9	Total number of applicants on the Live Register	**37,090**
9.a	Total below matric & others	**14,608**
	i. Below Matric including illiterates (general)	14,102

	ii. I.T.I passed certificate holders	224
	iii. Non-I.T.I (certificate) holders	41
	iv. Typist (below matric)	146
	v. Driving license holders	95
9.b	Total matriculates	**13,552**
	i. Matriculates (general)	13,180
	ii. I.T.I passed certificate holders	114
	iii. Non-I.T.I (certificate) holders	38
	iv. Matriculate stenographers	73
	v. Matriculate typist	147
9.c	Total pre-university	**5,398**
	i. P.U passed (general)	5,319
	ii P.U passed stenographers	27
	iii. P.U passed typist	52
9.d	Total graduates	**2,972**
	i. Graduates (general)	2,722
	ii. Technical degrees	185
	iii. Graduate stenographers	37
	iv. Graduate typist	28
9.e	Total post-graduates	**197**
9.f	Diploma Holders	**363**
10	Total men	**28,058**
11	Total women	**9,032**

Source: Directorate of Employment & Craftsmen Training, Nagaland.

The total number of applicants on the Live Register as on 31st December 2000 is 37,090, out of which 28,058 are men and 9,032 are women applicants. And this indicates that the male applicants constitute about 75.65 per cent, which is three times larger than the female applicants. This proportion brings into the mind a few questions. One clear reason could be that women are least bothered to get registered on the Live Register because they are not worried as much as the men about unemployment. Thus unemployment affects men at a higher rate, or men are always under higher pressure to get a job.

The total number of below matric & others is 14,608, of which - below matric including illiterate (general) = 14,102, I.T.I passed certificate holders = 114, Non-I.T.I (certificate) holders = 38, below matric typist = 146, driving license holders = 95. Again, there are 13'552 total matriculates, of which 13,180 are matriculates (general), 114 I.T.I passed certificate holders, 38 Non-I.T.I (certificate) holders, 73 matriculate stenographers, and 147 matriculate typist. There are also the total 5,398 pre-university applicants of which, 5,319 are P.U. passed (general), 27 P.U passed stenographers, and 52 P.U passed typist. Again, out of the total 2,972 graduates, 2,722 are graduates (general), 185 are technical graduates, 37 are graduate stenographers, and 28 graduate typist. And finally, there are 197 post-graduates remaining on the Live Register. Thus from the table, we have 22,119 total educated job seekers i.e. matriculate & matriculate above.

The description also highlights that, among these registered unemployed besides general degrees has also undertaken special training programmes like typists, I.T.I, non-I.T.I, stenographer, etc. From all the categories (educational qualification basis), we have the total 382 typist, 338 I.T.I passed (certificate) holders, 79 non-I.T.I (certificate) holders, 137 stenographers, and also 95 driving license holders. This also illustrates that, though the government in order to enhance their chances of getting jobs provides such training facilities, yet, it does not guarantee them any job, defeating the purpose of it. The educated job seekers (matric plus) constitute about 59.64 per cent of the total applicants on the Live Register, thus comprising a major section of the unemployed.

In this study, reaching the magnitude and trend of unemployment of the educated youth in Kohima District as well as the whole state of Nagaland, the data and figures of 10 years from 1991 to 2000 has been taken. And all these figures are as recorded in the Employment Exchanges at the end of every year respectively i.e. 31st December.

Table 2.2 gives the magnitude and trend of the unemployment in Nagaland from 1991 to 2000. The number of job seekers on the

Live Register of the Employment Exchange has increased from 22,069 in 1991 to 24,999 in 1995, which further increased to 37,090 at the end of December 2000. The Table reveals the increasing trend that the number of job seekers has gone up from 22.06 thousands in 1991 to 37.09 thousands in 2000 at an increased percentage of 68.06 (taking 1991 as the base). And the number of job seekers in the state is tended to increase along with the population growth (e.g. 12 lakhs in 1991 to 19 lakhs in 2001), along with yearly addition of educated with varying degrees from different institutions and the corresponding un-expanding job scenario. Unemployment is also related to the economic situation. The expansion of job seekers also means lack of job creation by the government, which could also mean lack of funds, resources, etc.

Table 2.2
Trend of Unemployment in Nagaland (1991-2000)
Base 1991=100

Year	No. of Unemployed	Percentage
1991	22,069	-
1992	22,396	1.48
1993	24,449	10.78
1994	25,849	17.13
1995	24,999	13.28
1996	20,655	-6.49
1997	21,643	-1.93
1998	27,752	25.75
1999	35,463	60.69
2000	37,090	68.06

Sources: 1. Directorate of Employment and Craftsmen Training, Nagaland.
2. Annual Administrative Report.

As given in the Table, the number of job seekers on the Live Register has decreased to 20,655 (-6.41 per cent) and 21,643 (-1.93 per cent) in the years 1996 and 1997 respectively. This could indicate the success of the government in reducing the number of job seekers through creation of employment opportunities to the unemployed.

From Table 2.3, we find the number of yearly registrations; vacancies notified yearly, placements made yearly and the percentage increase/decrease on the Live Register over the preceding year. From this, we also find out the number of vacancies notified, vacancies filled in as against the number of job seekers. From column 2 of the Table, we find out that the number of Employment Exchanges remained same as 07 in all these years i.e. 1991-2000. In other words, all the 07 districts have 01 Employment Exchange each and not more. The government does not seem to be interested in creating more exchanges than it has in the last 10 years. Again, the credibility of the functioning of some of these exchanges has become questionable.

The column 3 of the Table states that there are 6,081 registrations made in the year 1991 which has increased over the next three years, but decreased to 4,580 in 1995, which again increases to 13,241 in 1999, but decreases to 8,980 in 2000. It shows there is no uniformity in the yearly registrations made during the last 10 years. There has been a steady increase of registrations in the years 1992, 1993 and 1994 corresponding to the steady increase of the total unemployed on the Live Register. The year 1995, show decrease alarmingly even below the base year 1991. The years 1998 and 1999 shows high rate of registrations, which also highlights the effective-positive response of the educated to the Employment Exchange.

In 1991, as against 22,069 registered job seekers, only 1,347 vacancies are notified and 225 placements are made through the Employment Exchange. This data on placements indicate that for one job, the number of unemployed persons in the state is 98. In 1995 as against 24,991 registered job seekers, 1,197 vacancies are notified, 87 placements are made, indicating 287 persons for one job. In 2000, as against 37,090 registered job seekers, only 339 vacancies are notified and 73 placements are made through the Employment Exchange, thus indicating 508 persons for a single job. Consequently, the probability of a person getting a job through the Employment Exchange is very low. As in 2000, where 508

Table 2.3

Number of yearly registrations, vacancies notified, placements made, and the number of job seekers on the live register in Nagaland.(1991 - 2000)

Year	No. of Employment Exchanges at end of the year	Registrations made during the year	Vacancies Notified	Placements (through employment exchange)	Live Register at the end of the year	% Increase / decrease on Live Register over the previous year	No. of unemployed persons for 1 job
1	2	3	4	5	6	7	8
1991	07	6081	1347	225	22,069	-	98
1992	07	6168	1429	341	22,396	1.48	66
1993	07	6275	790	100	24,449	9.17	244
1994	07	8782	1322	139	25,849	5.73	186
1995	07	4580	1197	87	24,991	- 3.32	287
1996	07	7704	508	100	20,655	-17.35	207
1997	07	7471	325	111	21,643	4.78	195
1998	07	10,540	448	99	27,752	28.23	280
1999	07	13,241	110	131	35,463	27.79	271
2000	07	8,980	339	73	37,090	4.59	508

Source: Directorate of Employment and Craftsmen Training, Nagaland.

persons have to fight for a single job, only one person will get the job while 507 will be left without any job. Now the question arises what will happen to these 507. What will they do to earn a living? Will they remain silent especially when the selection is not fair? Whom do they blame for not getting a job? The Table gives that the number of vacancies notified, and placements made has declined rapidly, in spite of the increasing trend of unemployment. It clearly indicates the seriousness of the problem where in 1991, 98 persons for one job has increased to 508 for one single job in 2000. Again the vacancies notified to the Employment Exchange and the vacancies filled in vary widely indicating that candidates from the open market fill in the number of notified vacancies. Thus in this manner the very purpose of the Exchange for which it has been started got defeated. In addition, this has retarded the unemployed to do registration with the Exchanges.

The Table also gives the percentage of yearly increase or decrease of total unemployment on the Live Register over the previous year. It has increased by a percentage of 1.48 per cent in 1992 over the previous year i.e. 1991, increased by 9.17 per cent in 1993 over the previous year i.e. 1992, increased by 5.73 per cent in 1994, decreased by -3.32 per cent in 1995, again decreased by -17.35 per cent in 1996, increased by 4.78 per cent in 1997, increased alarmingly by 28.23 per cent in 1998, again highly increased by 27.79 per cent in 1999, and slightly increased by 4.59 per cent in 2000 over the previous year, i.e. 1999. Except the years 1995 and 1996, we could also see the increasing percentage of unemployment over the preceding year in all the eight remaining years. The statistics also depicts that though the government is able to confine the figure at around 20 thousands up to 1998, yet the figures are alarmingly high in the years 1999 and 2000. It depicts that the government is not able to restrict the figures anymore in the last 2 years, which also gives an alarm signal of the seriousness of the problem.

As given in Table 2.4, the number of educated unemployed has increased over the last 10 years. It increased from 10,534 in 1991 to 13,421 in 1995, which further increased to 22,119 in 2000. Thus taking the year 1991 as the base, the increased percentage, which is 27.41 per cent in 1995, has risen to 109.98 per cent in 2000.

Table 2.4
Applicants remaining on the Live Register on Employment Exchange in Nagaland (1991 - 2000)

Year	Matric &above	Graduates &above	Total Educated Job Seekers Matric Plus (2 + 3)	Percentage Base 1991 = 100	Below matric & others	Total Job Seekers on Live Register at the end of the) Year. (4 + 6)	% share of educated in total unemployed
1	2	3	4	5	6	7	8
1991	9388	1146	10,534	-	11,535	22,069	47.73
1992	10,164	1464	11,628	10.39	10,768	22,396	51.92
1993	11,133	1767	12,900	22.46	11,549	24,449	52.76
1994	11,857	1780	13,637	29.46	12,212	25,849	52.76
1995	11,811	1610	13,421	27.41	11,570	24,991	53.70
1996	10,652	2688	13,340	26.64	7,315	20,655	64.58
1997	11,623	2783	14,406	36.76	7,237	21,643	66.56
1998	16,256	3254	19,510	85.21	8,242	27,752	70.30
1999	18,616	2958	21,574	104.80	13,889	35,463	60.84
2000	18,950	3169	22,119	109.98	14,971	37,090	59.64

Source: 1. Directorate of Employment and Craftsmen Training, Nagaland.
2. Annual Administrative Report.

Comparatively, in the last 10 years, the educated unemployed, which has increased at the percentage of 109.98 per cent is much higher than the increased percentage of the total unemployed which is 68.06 per cent (taking 1991 as the base). And this is justified if we go along by the expanding number of students that are produced from various schools, colleges and institutions. The number of educated unemployed will rapidly emerge like large armies, if lasting solutions to unemployment is not brought in.

Obviously, the highest number of educated unemployed are below graduates i.e. matric & above in all these 10 years. The number of matric & above in 1991 is 9,388 which constitutes 89.12 per cent of the total educated unemployed; in 1995 their total number is 11,811 which constitutes 88.00 per cent; in 2000 their total number is 18,950 constituting 85.67 per cent of the total educated unemployed. The number of educated graduates & above is 1,146 in 1991, which constitutes only 10.87 per cent of the total educated unemployed; it is 1,610 in 1995 constituting 11.99 per cent; and it is 3,169 in 2000 constituting about 14.33 per cent. As discussed above, the educated unemployed on the Live Register has been broadly divided into two sections with graduates as the dividing line, i.e. i) below graduates (matric plus but below graduates) and, ii) graduates and above. And it is essential to note that, though the major concentration of educated unemployment are still below graduates, yet this proportion steadily decreases every year. On the other hand, the number of educated graduates & above have been steadily increasing in the last 10 years. Therefore, the trend depicts the problem to be tilted towards educated graduates & above in the near future.

From Table 2.4 we can also study the percentage share of educated in total unemployed. And, over the period 1991 to 2000, we can see the steady - increasing share of educated unemployed youth as against the overall unemployment. The educated unemployed youth which constitutes 47.73 per cent of total unemployed in 1991, has risen to 51.92 per cent in 1992, to 52.76 per cent in 1993, remained same as 52.76 per cent in 1994, again risen to 53.70 per cent in 1995, to 64.58 per cent in 1996, to 66.56 per cent in 1997, to 70.30 per cent in 1998, but decreased to 60.84

per cent in 1999, decreased to 59.64 per cent in 2000. The Table reveals that in all these years the percentage share of educated in total unemployed is never below 50.00 per cent, except in the year 1991, which is 47.73 per cent. Again since 1996, the percentage share of educated is above 60.00 per cent. Therefore, the problem of unemployment in the state is more or less, simply the problem of educated unemployed youth. It also means the unemployed in the state, are represented by the educated youth. This representation looks more serious for they are intelligent people - who can do more harm to the security and stability of the state. And therefore, the state policy makers / planners in making any solution should keep in mind that they are solving the problem of educated youth.

II. MAGNITUDE AND TREND - KOHIMA DISTRICT:

The data and figures that have been collected for Kohima District at the time of the study also included Dimapur District (presently) in its jurisdiction.

Table 2.5 gives the number of yearly registrations, placements made through Employment Exchanges, total number of job seekers on the Live Register, percentage of increase or decrease on Live Register over the previous year, and the number of unemployed persons for one single job in the District over the periods 1991 - 2000.

There is only 01 Employment Exchange in the District, right from 1991 to 2000. But in addition, being the capital, the Directorate of Employment and Craftsmen Training is in Kohima. The number of job seekers on the Live Register in the District has increased from 12,064 in 1991 to 17,296 at the end of December 2000, at the rate of 43.37 per cent (taking 1991 as base). This shows that in 10 years (i.e. 1991 - 2000) only 5,232 unemployed youth are added to the figure of 1991 at an annual growth rate of 4.34 per cent. Thus comparatively the district has done better than the whole state in restricting the growth of unemployment. Perhaps the unemployed in the district are doing better than their counterparts from the other districts in grabbing the job opportunities that avails, and consequently reduced the unemployed figure in the district. As given in the Table, 3,162 registrations are made in the year 1991,

Table 2.5

Number of Yearly Registrations, Vacancies Notified, Placements made, and the number of job seekers on the Live Register on Regional Employment Exchange, Kohima - Kohima District. (1991 - 2000)

Year	No. of Employment Exchanges at the end of the year	Registrations made during the year	Vacancies Notified	Placements made(through employment exchange)	Live Register at the end of the year	% Increase/ decrease on Live Register over the previous year	No. of unemployed persons for 1 job
1	2	3	4	5	6	7	8
1991	01	3162	617	82	12,064	-	147
1992	01	3493	465	95	11,666	-3.30	123
1993	01	3423	276	28	12,871	10.33	460
1994	01	3209	292	45	13,253	2.97	295
1995	01	2604	159	63	12,889	-2.75	205
1996	01	4787	203	26	15,699	21.80	604
1997	01	3892	171	81	12,361	-21.26	153
1998	01	5616	133	63	15,450	24.99	245
1999	01	5472	52	45	17,449	13.26	388
2000	01	4186	119	66	17,296	- 0.88	262

Source: Regional Employment Exchange, Kohima.

which remains almost constant for the next three years. But, only 2,604 registrations are made in the year 1996. In 2000, there are 4,186 registrations made. These registrations are not all-fresh registrations, but it also includes renewals, which has to be done after every three years, if the person is still unemployed without any job.

In 1991, as against 12,064 registered job seekers, only 617 vacancies are notified and 82 placements are made through the Employment Exchange. This data on placements indicate that for one single job, the number of unemployed persons is 147. Again in 1995, as against 12,889 registered job seekers, only 159 vacancies are notified and 63 placements are made through the Employment Exchange, indicating 205 unemployed persons for one single job. In 2000, as against 17,296 registered job seekers, only 119 vacancies are notified and 66 placements are made which indicates that for one single job, there are 262 persons against it. Again in the same year, only 73 placements are made in the whole state, indicating thus, all the placements are made through Kohima Employment Exchange itself with 66 placements (i.e. 90.41 per cent). In 1992, 95 placements (the highest in 10 years) has been made, indicating still 123 persons for a single job; while in 1996, only 26 placements (the lowest in 10 years) against 15,699 registered job seekers are made, indicating the highest (in 10 years) 604 persons to fight for a single job. The data for other years can be seen from the same Table. Consequently, the probability of an unemployed person getting a job through the Employment Exchange is very low. The number of notified vacancies and placements made has been decreasing in spite of the increasing trend of unemployment in the district. The number of vacancies notified and the placements made through the Exchange has been decreasing in spite of the increasing trend of unemployment in the district. Moreover, the vacancies notified and placements made through the exchange do not tally, which clearly indicates that jobs are filled-in from the open market. And the Employment Exchanges will never be effective until and unless vacant jobs of all the departments are compulsorily notified through the exchanges. If we calculate by the placement figures through the exchanges, which are minimal, the exchanges are only helping the unemployed to get registered and not more than that.

The percentage of yearly increase or decrease of total unemployment on Live Register over the previous year is also given in Table 2.5. It has decreased by a percentage of -3.30 per cent in 1992 from the previous year of 1991, but increased by a percentage of 10.33 per cent in 1993 which further increased by 2.97 per cent in 1994, again decreased by -2.75 per cent in 1995, increased by 21.80 per cent in 1996, decreased by -21.26 per cent in 1997, increased by 24.99 per cent in 1998, increased by 13.26 per cent in 1999, but decreased by -0.88 per cent in 2000 over the year 1999. Therefore as shown, the number of unemployed on the Live Register has been fluctuating and not uniformly increasing or decreasing. In these 10 years, it has increased five times and decreased four times over the previous year.

Table 2.6

Applicants remaining on the Live Register on Regional Employment Exchange of Kohima District and percentage share of Educated in Total Unemployed. (1991 – 2000)

Year	Total (Registered) Job seekers	Below Matric &others	Educated Job Seekers (matriculation plus)	Percentage Base 1991 = 100	% share educated in toatl unemployed
1	2	3	4	5	6
1991	12,064	5731	6,333	-	52.50
1992	11,666	5245	6,421	1.39	55.04
1993	12,871	5876	6,995	10.45	54.35
1994	13,253	6416	6,837	7.96	51.59
1995	12,889	6296	6,593	4.11	51.15
1996	15,699	7811	7,888	24.55	50.25
1997	12,361	3750	8,6113	5.97	69.66
1998	15,450	4066	11,384	79.76	73.68
1999	17,449	4811	12,638	99.56	72.43
2000	17,296	4466	12,690	100.39	73.37

Source: Regional Employment Exchange, Kohima.

As shown in Table 2.6, the number of educated unemployment in Kohima District has increased in the last 10 years. It has increased from 6,333 in 1991 at an increased percentage of 24.55 per cent to 7,888 in 1996. This has further increased to 12,690 in 2000 at an increased percentage of 100.39 per cent. Thus in 10 years, the educated unemployed youth of Kohima District has increased from 6,333 to 12,638. It is observed that the number of job seekers in the district has increased only at the rate of 43.37 per cent (1991-2000), while the educated unemployed youth of the same district has increased at the rate of 100.39 per cent. As given in the Table, we can also see the fast and steep increasing trend from 1996 to 2000. These years co-incidentally have seen the blooming up of many schools and colleges in the district, which relatively resulted in producing students of varying degrees and qualifications.

The number of unemployment (below matric & others) in Kohima District shows a steady increase from 1991 to 1996. It has increased from 5,731 in 1991 to 7,811 in 1996 at the increased rate of 36.29 per cent, i.e. by taking 1991 as the base. This steady increase can be reflected as the increasing number of school dropouts in the district in these years. However the number of unemployment in this category in the years 1997,1998, 1999, and 2000 shows below the total number of the base year. Thus the number stands at 4,466 at a decreased rate of -22.07 per cent from the base year 1991. Moreover, education is also related with the economy of the society, the family, etc. There are families who cannot afford their children to complete their studies. On the other hand, some students can easily afford but does not continue with their education. The decreased rate of -22.07 per cent (in the category below matric & others) can be depicted as the improved economy of the district, though it cannot be the sole reason.

The percentage share of educated unemployed in total unemployed from 1991 to 2000 is also given in the same Table i.e. Table 2.6. The educated unemployed youth constituting 52.50 per cent of total unemployed in 1991 has risen to 73.37 per cent in 2000. However, the increasing trend is not uniformly continuous. The percentage share of educated unemployed in 1992 is 55.04 per cent, in 1993 it is 54.35 per cent, in 1994 it is 51.59 per cent, in

1995 it is 51.15 per cent, in 1996 it is 50.25 per cent, in 1997 it is 69.66 per cent, in 1998 it is 73.68 per cent, and 1999 it is 72.43 per cent. The percentage share of educated unemployed reveals that in the last 10 years, its share is always above 50.00 percent. The percentage share of educated unemployed in total unemployed has rapidly increased from 1997 onwards which tells the seriousness of unemployment among the educated youth. The above discussion also depicts that more attention has to be given to the educated unemployed youth. The proportion of educated against the total unemployed in the district is much higher than the corresponding percentage of the whole state. With 73.37 per cent of the educated unemployed youth against the total unemployment is an imbalance picture between the output and the input. The government seems to be fully interested in encouraging education for all without creating subsequent job opportunities. In addition, it results in severe consequences with many educated to remain unemployed finding their respective degrees useless.

As shown in Table 2.7, the highest number of educated unemployed in Kohima District in all these years are matriculates, followed by pre-university (10+2), graduates, and post-graduates respectively. According to the data of 1991, matriculates constitute 72.08 per cent, pre-university constitutes 14.62 per cent, graduates constitute 12.17 per cent and post-graduates constitute 1.12 per cent of the total educated unemployed youth. In the year 2000, matriculates constituted about 60.78 per cent, pre-university constituted 23.46 per cent, graduates constituted 14.59 per cent, and post-graduates constituted about 1.17 per cent of the total educated unemployed in the district. Though the major concentrations of educated unemployed are in the matriculate' category, the percentage share has been steadily decreasing in the last 10 years as revealed by the data in the Table. On the other hand, the percentage share of pre-university, graduates and post-graduates - all show a steady increase in these 10 years. This is related with the increase number of educational institutions and the consequent bulging of students in higher studies.

Table 2.7 also gives separate data for males and females of different qualifications. It has shown that in all the years i.e.

Table 2.7

Educated applicants (matriculation plus) remaining on the Live Register on Regional Employment Exchange, Kohima - of Kohima District and percentage increase over the previous year. (1991 - 2000)

Year	Matriculate		Pre-University		Graduate		Post-Graduate		Total Male	Total Female	Total Educated (matric-plus) (6 + 7)	% increase of Educated over the previous year
1	2		3		4		5		6	7	8	9
	M	F	M	F	M	F	M	F				
1991	2845	1720	670	256	537	234	40	31	4092	2241	6,333	-
1992	2763	1487	815	355	628	295	36	42	4242	2179	6,421	1.39
1993	2898	1542	1016	398	735	312	42	52	4691	2304	6,995	8.94
1994	2753	1363	965	519	832	323	38	44	4588	2249	6,837	-2.26
1995	2540	1273	1124	516	795	286	25	34	4484	2109	6,593	-3.57
1996	2567	1366	1265	736	1193	635	69	57	5094	2794	7,888	19.64
1997	3012	1472	1336	799	1186	684	62	60	5596	3015	8,611	9.17
1998	4065	2097	1778	1153	1306	851	69	65	7218	4166	11,384	32.30
1999	5055	2458	1907	1132	1228	741	63	54	8253	4385	12,638	11.01
2000	5186	2527	1825	1152	1131	720	71	78	8213	4477	12,690	0.41

Source: Regional Employment Exchange, Kohima.

1991-2000, in the different qualification levels except with post-graduates, men constitute the larger proposition than women do. But, with post-graduates, men as well as women outnumber each other in different years. According to this data, it could be true that women are not fairing as good as men at lower levels, but are doing as good as men at higher levels of education.

The number of matriculates which is 4,565 in 1991 has decreased over the next 6 years, but increased to 6,162 in 1998, and again increased to 7,513 in 1999, further increased to 7,713 in 2000 at an increased percentage of 68.96 per cent (base 1991 = 100). The educated unemployed youth with pre-university qualification has shown at first steady, but later on sharp increase. It has increased from 926 in 1991 to 1,640 in 1995, to 2,977 in 2000 at an increased rate of 221.49 per cent. The number of graduates has increased from 771 in 1991 to 1,081 in 1995, to 1,851 in 2000 at an increased rate of 140.08 per cent (base 1991 = 100). The number of post-graduates registered at the Employment Exchange, Kohima is not uniform. The figure which is 71 in 1991, has come down as low as 59 in 1995, and again risen to 149 in 2000 at an increased rate of 109.86 per cent (base 1991 = 100). Therefore, we find educated unemployment in the category of pre-university to have been increased the most with an increased rate of 221.49 per cent, followed by graduates with an increased rate of 140.08 per cent.

The total number of educated unemployed males always constituted the larger proportion than females. As given in column 6 and column 7 of Table 2.7, the total males in 1991 was 4,092 constituting 64.61 percent of the total educated unemployed, whereas the total females was only 2,241 which constituted 35.39 percent. In 2000, the number of total males was 8,213 which constituted 64.72 percent and the total females was 4,477, constituted about 35.28 percent. According to 1991 census, the population ratio (male: female) in the state stands as 53.02:46.98 and the sex ratio was 886 females for 1000 males. Again, the literacy rate according to 1991 census is 67.62 per cent males and 54.75 per cent females. Now relating to these facts, the total educated unemployed females constituting only 35.28 per cent in 2000 pose a dubious question the mind. Either men are totally outnumbering the women in educational institutions or the educated women are least interested in registering in the Employment Exchanges. It can be concluded that the responsibility of earning and making a living after education lies on men because of which men are much more worried and concerned for jobs, which also means registration in the Employment Exchanges.

Table 2.7 also gives the percentage of increase or decrease of educated unemployed over the previous years in Kohima District of Nagaland, basing on the data of Regional Employment Exchange, Kohima. It has increased from 6,333 in 1991 at an increased rate of 1.39 per cent to 6,421 in 1992, increased to 6,995 at the rate of 8.94 per cent in 1993, but decreased to 6,837 at the rate of -2.26 per cent in 1994, again decreased to 6,593 at the rate of -3.57 per cent in 1995, has risen to 7,888 at the rate of 19.64 per cent in 1996, increased to 8,611 at the rate of 9.17 per cent in 1997, further risen to 11,384 at the rate of 32.30 per cent in 1998, risen to 12,638 at the rate of 11.01 per cent in 1999, and has risen to 12,690 at the increased rate of 0.41 per cent in 2000 over the previous year. The data depicts that there is no uniformity in the percentage of yearly increase in this study of 10 years. In some years it has increased as high as 32.30 per cent over the previous year, while it has also increased as low as 0.41 per cent in some other years. Again in the years 1994 and 1995, educated unemployed has decreased over the respective previous year. Thus in these two years the total educated unemployed which is 6,995 in 1993 has reduced to 6,593 in 1995. It is also difficult to attribute the reduction of unemployment as a success to the government or Employment Exchange to have generated employment to the unemployed youth. Because the data on placements made through the Exchanges is not significant as such. In the same years the placements made could not read as indications of the justification by generating employment to reduce the figures.

Table 2.8 has highlighted the percentage share of Kohima District unemployment as against the whole state of Nagaland. The Table also gives the percentage share of Kohima District educated unemployed as against the state for the last 10 years. And as given

Table 2.8

Percentage Share of Kohima District - total Unemployed (all), total Educated Unemployed - against the State (Nagaland) total Unemployed, total Educated Unemployed respectively on Live Register (1991 - 2000)

Year	Total Unemployed (Kohima District)	Total Unemployed (Nagaland)	% share of Kohima District Total Unemployed against the state	Total Educated Unemployed (Kohima District)	Total Educated Unemployed (Nagaland)	% share of Kohima District Educated Unemployed against the state
1	2	3	4	5	6	7
1991	12,064	22,069	54.66	6,333	10,534	60.12
1992	11,666	22,396	52.09	6,421	11,628	55.22
1993	12,871	24,449	52.64	6,995	12,900	54.22
1994	13,253	25,849	51.27	6,837	13,637	50.14
1995	12,889	24,991	51.57	6,593	13,421	49.12
1996	15,699	20,655	76.01	7,888	13,340	59.13
1997	12,361	21,643	57.11	8,611	14,406	59.77
1998	15,450	27,752	55.67	11,384	19,510	58.35
1999	17,449	35,463	48.77	12,638	21,574	58.58
2000	17,296	37,090	46.63	12,690	22,119	57.37

Source: 1. Regional Employment Exchange, Kohima.
2. Directorate of Employment and Craftsmen Training, Nagaland.

in the Table, the trend of the percentage share is not uniform i.e. it increases or decreases at different years.

The percentage share of Kohima District total unemployed against the state total unemployed is 54.66 per cent in 1991, 52.09 per cent in 1992, 52.64 per cent in 1993, 51.27 per cent in 1994, 51.57 per cent in 1995, 76.01 per cent in 1996, 57.11 per cent in 1997, 55.67 per cent in 1998, and 48.77 per cent in 1999, and 46.63 per cent in 2000. This percentage of Kohima district total unemployed is the highest in the year 1996 with 76.01 per cent, which is much higher than all the other years. The fact is, not only due to the increase of Kohima district total unemployed over the previous year (21.80 per cent) but also due to the decrease of the state total unemployed over the previous year (-17.35 per cent), which is also the lowest figure in 10 years. Again, the percentage share of Kohima district unemployed has shown the lowest in the year 2000 with only 46.63 per cent. This indicates that the disease of unemployment seems to be taking a new trend evenly spreading to the other districts, which is previously more or less the monopoly issue with the capital district as revealed by the Table. However, it should be noted that still almost half of the total registered unemployed are from the Kohima district alone. In other words, the maximum concentrations of registered unemployed are from the capital itself.

The percentage share of Kohima District total educated unemployed against the state total educated unemployed is 60.12 per cent in 1991, 55.22 per cent in 1992, 54.22 per cent in 1993, 50.14 per cent in 1994, 49.12 per cent in 1995, 59.13 per cent in 1996, 59.77 per cent in 1997, 58.35 per cent in 1998, 58.58 per cent in 1999 and 57.37 per cent in 2000. The district percentage share of educated unemployed as revealed is even higher, with its share constantly above 50 per cent in all these years except the year 1995, which is only 49.12 per cent. The problem of the educated unemployed in the district up to 2000 stands as serious as the beginning i.e. base year 1991. The data reveals that a large 57.37 per cent of the educated unemployed without any job in the state are concentrated in the district. It is quite possible that the youth from different districts prefers to stay in the capital after finishing studies to obtain jobs. Besides the capital town, the district also has the commercial town - Dimapur, which comes under the district at the time of study. Perhaps the educated unemployed youth moves to these two towns expecting better chances and opportunities for means of livelihood, if not the government job. The district percentage share of total unemployed justifies this assumption in 2000, which is only 46.63 per cent, whereas the district percentage share of educated unemployed is as high as 57.37 per cent.

Thus, to conclude, there is an alarming rise of unemployment among the educated youth in Nagaland. The problem of unemployment in the state is more or less, simply the problem of educated youth. Again, in spite of the increasing trend of unemployment, the number of vacancies and placement made has declined. The probability of an unemployed person to get a job in the state therefore is very low. It is necessary to note that more than half of the unemployed; educated unemployed has always concentrated in Kohima district alone.

This problem of unemployment badly affects the present Naga youth and the state as a whole. This is an issue with the youth, with the educated youth who are intelligent people, who can become dangerously vocal and influential not to accept any unenviable position lying down to give constant threat to the security and stability of the state. There cannot be social and political stability in the state, if its youth (considered to be the best of our human resources) are without work. The policy makers/planners have an urgent responsibility to device policies that may alleviate this problem and to bring out lasting solutions to unemployment. Unemployment should not be viewed as a 'risidual' problem to be tackled after the other problems have been solved, but as the 'primary' problem.

3

Socio-Economic Background

In the previous chapter we have discussed the magnitude and trend of unemployment in the state, the trend of educated unemployment in the capital district. This present chapter studies the personal characteristics of the respondents, as it is imperative to know, in order to draw out certain basic conclusions about the study. The personal characteristics of the respondents such as - sex composition, faculty, age-structure and marital status, occupational status of the father, educational attainment of parents, father's income and family's total income, type and size of family, etc are studied and recorded accordingly. These characteristics are summarized in the following manner.

i. Sex:

Sex is dichotomously categorized as a) male and b) female. Sex of the respondent in this study as expected, has a differential impact, because of the differences in sex role socialization of males and females. Normatively, males are expected to earn and make a living, whereas the primary obligation of females is to assume the roles of a wife and a mother. Hence, unemployment is more stressful to males than females. (Chakrapani, 1995).

The number of male respondents' (121) in the sample is almost twice that of the female respondents' (70). And among the male respondents there are 06 (40.00%) matriculates, 32 (72.73%) pre-university, 55 (67.90(%) graduates, and 28 (54.90%) post-graduates. (Table 3.1). Therefore, the corresponding female respondents are

Table 3.1
Sample composition by educational level, sex, and course of study

Educational Level	Sex												Total (M + F) (N =191)
	Males (N = 121)						Females (N = 70)						
1 Matric	06						09						**(6+9)=15**
2 Pre-University	**A** 10		**S** 09		**C** 13		**A** 05		**S** 05		**C** 02		**(32+12) = 44**
3 Graduate	**A**	**S**	**C**	**L**	**M**	**E**	**A**	**S**	**C**	**L**	**M**	**E**	**(55+26)=81**
	06	09	12	07	10	11	09	05	03	05	01	03	
4 Post-Graduate	04	05	09	07	01	02	10	09	02	00	02	00	**(28+23)=51**
Total	**A**	**S**	**C**	**L**	**M**	**E**	**A**	**S**	**C**	**L**	**M**	**E**	**(121+70)=191**
	20	23	34	14	11	13	24	19	07	05	03	03	

Note: (A = arts, S = science, C = commerce, L = law, M = medicine, E = engineering).
(M = Male, F = Female, N = Total Number).

09 (60.00%) matriculates, 12 (27.27%) pre-university, 26 (32.10%) graduates, and 23 (45.10%) post-graduates.

It indicates that except in the matriculates' category, the sample has more male respondents. The total sample contains 63.35 per cent male and 36.65 per cent female educated unemployed youth. However this sex-sample is randomly selected and is disproportionate, which cannot be used for subsequent analysis.

ii. Faculty:

Breaking up the sample, according to faculty it indicates that 44 (23.04%) respondents are from the arts faculty, 42 (21.99%) from the science faculty, 41 (21.47%) from the commerce faculty, 19 (9.95%) from the law faculty, 16 (8.38%) from the engineering faculty and 14 (7.33%) from the medicine faculty. The faculty-wise break up of the sample is done purposively as already discussed in the first chapter which is sorted out as 45 each from the arts, science and commerce group, 30 each from the law, medicine, and engineering group. Therefore, the final response rate in each group is, arts - 44 (97.78%), science - 42 (93.33%), commerce - 41 (91.11%), law - 19 (63.33%), medicine - 14 (46.67%), and engineering - 16 (53.33%). It indicates the most successful responses from the arts group while the least successful response is from the medicine group, which is less than 50.00 per cent.

Again, faculty and sex-wise distribution of the sample indicates that 20 (45.45%) of the respondents in the arts group are males, 23 (54.76%) in the science faculty, 34 (82.93%) in the commerce faculty, 14 (73.68%) in the law faculty, 11 (78.57%) in medicine and 13 (81.25%) in the engineering faculty are males. And the corresponding sample shows that 24 (54.55%) of the respondents in the arts group are females, 19 (45.24%) females in the science faculty, 07 (17.07%) females in the commerce faculty, 05 (26.32%) females in the law faculty, 03 (21.43%) in the medicine and 03 (18.75%) females in the engineering faculty. Thus, the analysis indicates a high percentage of males in all the 5 faculties, except the arts faculty, which indicates a high 24 (54.55%) of females. The high percentage of females in the arts faculty and males in commerce, engineering, medicine and law faculty may represent the traditional interests of male and female students. This may also represent the importance given to male students. This can be reflected upon the bringing up of children in the families, and the mental preparation of children in the society. However, it should be noted that the female candidates do better according to the recent performances in various examinations though the quantity is still enjoyed by the male.

iii. Age:

Age gives a clue about the stage of development of the personality. It is assumed that in a certain age, the person should achieve things, in form of education, marital status, employment, etc. Since the process of socialization is correlated with the age, to study the age structure of respondents is of utmost importance for the purpose of the research (Bajpai, 1992).

In this research study, the youth age group (bracketed as 15-34) is broken up into four sub - groups a) 15-19, b) 20-24, c) 25-29, and d) 30-34. Table 3.2 gives a complete idea of the age structure of the respondents.

The table denotes, in the matriculate category, 07 (46.67%) respondent youth belongs to 15-19 years age group, another 07 (46.67%) in 20-24 years age group, 01 (6.66%) in 25-29 years age group, and no respondent youth in 30-34 years age group. The mean age group of this category is 20.00 years, while mode (highest frequency) denotes (15 - 19) and (20 - 24) year age group as the most frequent category. In the pre-university category, 11 (25.00%) respondent youth belong to 15-19 years age group, 23 (52.27%) in 20-24 years age group, 06 (13.64%) in 25-29 years age group, and 04 (9.09%) in 30-34 years age group. The mean age group of this category is 22.34 years, while mode denotes (20 -24) year age group as the most frequent category. In the graduate category, 29 (35.80%) respondent youth belong to 20-24 years age group, 49 (60.49%) in 25-29 years age group, and 03 (3.70%) in 30-34 years age group, while there is no respondent in the age group of (15 - 19). The mean age group of this category is 25.40 years and mode denotes (25 - 29) year age group as the most frequent category. In the post-graduate category, 09 (17.65%) youth belong to 20-24

Table 3.2

Age distribution of the respondents on educational qualification basis

Age Group (Years)	Educational Qualification / Categories of Respondents												Grand Total (M + F)
	I Matric			II Pre-University			III Graduate			IV Post -Graduate			
	M	F	T	M	F	T	M	F	T	M	F	T	
15 - 19	03	04	07	08	03	11	0	0	0	0	0	0	**(11+07)=18**
20 - 24	02	05	07	15	08	23	15	14	29	04	05	09	**(36+32)=68**
25 - 29	01	0	01	05	01	06	37	12	49	23	17	40	**(66+30)=96**
30 - 34	0	0	0	04	0	04	03	0	03	01	01	02	**(08+01)=09**
Total	06	09	15	32	12	44	55	26	81	28	23	51	**(121+70)=191**
Mean		**20.00**			**22.34**			**25.40**			**26.31**		**24.51**

Note: (M = Male, F = Female, T = Total).
Mode = (25 - 29) age group.
Mean (male respondents) = 24.93 years
Mean (female respondents) = 23.79 year
Mean (Total) = 24.51 years.

years age group, 40 (78.43%) in 25-29 years age group and 02 (3.92%) in 30-34 years age group, but again there is no respondent in the age group of (15 - 19). The mean age group of this category is 26.31 years while mode denotes ((25 - 29) year age group as the most frequent category.

The mean age group of the four educational categories corresponds to their respective degrees. As the degree goes high, it involves higher number of years in our education system. Thus, in the matriculate' category we have only 01 respondent in the age group of (25-29) years and no respondent in (30-34) year age group. It is also obvious that there is no respondent in the age group of (15-19) years for both graduates and post-graduates category. However, in the pre-university category, it is surprising to note that there are 04 persons in the age group of (30-34) years, where even graduates and post-graduates have respectively 03 and 02 respondents each in the same age group. And all these 04 respondents are males.

The average mode period for the total sample is (25-29) age group and the mean age for the total sample is 24.51 years. The highest frequency i.e. 96 of the respondents in the age class of (25-29) years is obvious and understandable for two reasons: i) This study sample contains 132 (69.11%) graduates and post-graduates alone, who in the case of most Naga youth, usually completes their graduation and post-graduation between the age of 22 - 26 years. ii) This sample contains youth who remain unemployed after completing their studies, which add few more years to their age.

In the first category, matriculates, in 40.00 per cent respondent are male out of which 20.00 per cent are in the age group of (15-19) years, 13.33 per cent in (20-24) years age group and 6.67 per cent in the age group of (25-29) years. In the same category 26.67 per cent female respondents are in the age group of (15-19) years and 33.33 per cent female respondents are in the age group of (20-24) years accumulating 60.00 per cent female respondents in this category.

Pre-university category contains 27.28 per cent female respondents including 6.82 per cent in (15-19) years age group, 18.18 per cent in (20-24) years age group and 2.27 per cent in (25-

29) years age group. The male respondents have strength of 72.72 per cent on the category including 18.18 per cent in (15-19) years age group, 34.09 per cent in (20-24) years age group, 11.36 per cent in (25-29) years age group and (.09 per cent in the age group of (30-34) years.

Females form 32.10 per cent of the strength of graduates' category comprising 17.28 per cent in (20-24) years age group and 14.82 per cent in (25-29) years age group. The male respondents constitute to 67.90 per cent of the sample of this category representing 18.52 per cent in (20-24) years age group, 45.68 per cent in (25-29) years age group and 3.70 per cent in the age group of (30-34) years.

In the last category, post-graduates, 45.10 per cent respondents are female out of which 9.80 per cent are the age group of (20-24) years, 33.33 per cent in (25-29) years age group, and 1.96 per cent in (30-34) years age group. In the same category, 7.84 per cent male respondents are there in the age group of (20-24) years, 45.10 per cent male respondents in (15-19) years age group and 1.96 per cent male respondents are in the age group of (30-34) years accumulating 54.90 per cent male respondents in this category.

Thus, the mean average age of the male respondents is 24.93 years and that of the female is 23.79 years.

iv. Marital Status:

Marital status is the definite indicator of the man's liabilities in the society like that of Indians where only male folk go out for work bearing the liability of female partner in the life, as a custom. It rather adds to the burden of a man, manifold-social, psychological, familial, financial and adjustmental. Marriage indicates the perfection in life, but for an unemployed youth, it is an extra burden to bear upon one's head. (Bajpai, 1992).

Marital status is coded into four nominal categories: a) married, b) unmarried, c) divorced, and d) widow/widower. The cross-tabulated frequency data concerning the marital status vis-a-vis the educational status is shown in Table 3.3.

Table 3.3
Distribution of respondents by marital status

Marital Status	Matric (%)	Pre-University (%)	Graduates (%)	Post-Graduates (%)	Total (%)
1 Married	0	4.55 (02)	7.41 (06)	9.80 (05)	6.81 (13)
2 Unmarried	100.00 (15)	95.45 (42)	92.59 (75)	88.24 (45)	**92.67** **(177)**
3 Divorced	0	0	0	0.52 (01)	0.52 (01)
4 Widow/ Widower	0	0	0	0	0
Total	100.00 (15)	100.00 (44)	100.00 (81)	100.00 (51)	100.00 (191)

Note: Figures in parentheses are actual No. of respondents.

The Table depicts that in the matriculate' category all the 15 (100%) respondents are unmarried. In the pre-university category, only 02 (4.55%) respondents are married and 42 (95.45%) respondents are still unmarried. In the graduates' category, there are 06 (7.41%) respondents who are married and there are 75 (92.59%) respondents who belong to the unmarried category. In the last category, post-graduates, 05 (9.80%) respondents are married, 45 (88.24%) respondents are unmarried, while 01 (0.52%) respondent got married and divorced.

The unmarried respondents are thirteen times larger than the married respondents. Of the married respondents 02 (15.38%) belongs to pre-university category, 6 (46.15%0 respondents are graduates and 05 (38.46%) are post-graduates. And of the unmarried respondents 15 (8.47%) are from the matriculates' educational status, 42 (23.73%) are having pre-university educational status, 73 (42.37%) are graduates and 45 (25.42%) are post-graduates. Again, out of the total 191 respondents, 01 respondent is a divorcee, while the sample does not have any respondent in the widow/widower category.

Therefore, the data reveals that 6.81 (13) per cent of the sample contains married respondent, 92.67 (177) per cent are unmarried and 0.52 (01) per cent constitutes the divorced category. And this 92.67 per cent of the respondents in the unmarried category clearly indicates that it is an extra burden for an unemployed to get married to the already social, psychological and economic problems he/she is facing. An unemployed person prefers to stay as unmarried until and unless he/she gets a job. The study reveals that it is quite genuine that on completing studies, it is primary to get a job or be employed while marriage should be secondary irrespective of age. Moreover, it is also the tendency of parents to give their daughter to an employed groom.

v. Father's Occupation, Mother's Occupation:

Occupational and educational status of the family have a determining influence on a student' access to higher education in India. (Dhar, 1976). Family occupation suggests economic structure, and social status of the family in the society. It deciphers the means of livelihood of the family. Urban and rural background also plays an important role in judging the personality of a human being. Value system and behaviour patterns are also formed accordingly and future course of action for the youth is decided on the basis of their place of dwelling (Bajpai, 1992).

The occupational status of father and mother are grouped into 7 occupational categories as a) Professional / Technical, b) Administrative / Executive, c) Clerical Workers, d) Sales Workers / Business, e) Farmers / Craftsmen, f) Housewife (only for mother), g) Others. These occupational categories and the corresponding frequency distributions of respondents are reported in Table 3.4 given below. However, generalization to the population cannot be made on this basis, because of the lack of certainty of the representativeness of the sample.

Taking the total sample into account, 49 respondents or 25.65 per cent of the sample reported clerical workers as father's occupation, 42 respondents or 21.99 per cent reported administrative/ executive as father's occupation. The occupational category of others is reported by 38 respondents or 19.90 per cent. And the remaining 32.46 per cent approximately accounts for occupational categories like - professional / technical, sales workers / business, and farmers/ craftsmen.

Table 3.4
Distribution of (Educated Unemployed) Respondents by Father'sOccupation/Mother's Occupation.

Occupational status of Father/ Mother	Distribution of educated unemployed youth	
	Father	Mother
1 Professional/Technical	17 (8.90)	13 (6.81)
2 Administrative/Executive	42 (21.99)	09 (4.71)
3 Clerical workers	49 (25.65)	23 (12.04)
4 Sales workers/Business	20 (10.47)	07 (3.67)
5 Farmers/Craftsmen	25 (13.09)	37 (19.37)
6 Housewife		70 (36.65)
7 Other	38 (19.90)	32 (16.75)
Total	191(100.00)	191(100.00)

Note: Figures in the parentheses indicates %.

Of the seven occupational categories, 70 respondents or 36.65 per cent of the sample reported housewife as mother's occupation. And this alone account for approximately one-third of the total sample. The remaining two-third consisted of farmers / craftsmen (37, 19.37), others (32, 16.75), clerical workers (23, 12.04), professional / technical (13, 6.81), administrative / executive (09, 4.71) and sales workers / business (07, 3.67).

Therefore, the occupational status of father of the educated unemployed respondents as depicted above is distributed in all the seven occupational categories. In other words, the educated unemployed respondents are from all categories of classes - poor, middle, and rich class. Unemployment is not confined to only a particular section of people, but has penetrated to all the sections of the society. One-third of respondents' mothers as housewives depict that the economy of the family lies solely on the father. It can also be understood that; the father has the major responsibility for the maintenance of the family especially when the money/income is concerned.

However, it is not possible to conclude whether parent's occupation has anything to do with the magnitude or frequency of unemployment among the educated youth. (Chakrapani, 1995).

vi. Religion:

Religion forms the backbone of our systems and beliefs. Without understanding the religious beliefs prevailing in the society, we cannot understand the society. It, not merely, implies a relationship between men but also between man and some higher power. (MacIver, 1959). Green explains that religion performs three universal functions: *firstly*, it rationalizes and makes bearable individual suffering in the known world; *secondly*, it enhances self-importance and *thirdly*, it helps to knit the social values of a society into a cohesive whole. (Green, 1956).

The present study relates to human beings, human beings in problem - the problem of educated youth, and, therefore, it is obligatory to know also their religious beliefs in order to assess the aspirations, to highlight the problems, to study the attitudes and actions of the educated unemployed youth. Table 3.5 presents the religious structure of the respondents.

Table 3.5
Distribution of sample by Religion

Sl No	I Religion	II Number	III %
A	Christianity	183	**95.81**
B	Hindu	06	3.14
C	Muslim	00	0.00
D	Others	02	1.05

The table makes it evident that 183 respondents or approximately 96% of the total sample are Christians, while the rest 4% respondents are constituted by Hindus and others (which include paganism, etc). However, it has to be noted that no respondent of this sample belongs to the Muslim category.

Since it is Christian dominated, the majority of the respondents (96%) are Christians, though they come from different denominations. Again, the sample contains 183 Naga respondents from about fourteen different tribes of Nagaland and Manipur. There are 08 Non-Nagas in the sample out of which 02 are Christians and all 06 Hindus are Non-Nagas. Out of 183 Naga respondents, 181 respondents are Christians and 02 respondents follow the traditional pagan religion.

vii. Father's Education, Mother's Education:

Education is the preparation for life. A person learns about the ways and means of living through education and tries to apply the knowledge in the course of his/her life to earn their livelihood. Thus, in this study of socio-economic background, and study of the family background, it is imperative to know about the parent's educational status of the respondents.

The parent's educational status is grouped into 7 categories, which are studied separately for father and separately for mother. The sub-grouped 7 categories includes: a) illiterate / some home education, b) completed primary school, c) completed middle school, d) high school - not completed, e) completed high school / matriculated, f) completed intermediate / PU, g) BA / MA. Table 3.6 given below presents a unified picture of educational status of parents of the respondents.

The Table makes it evident that the fathers' of 58 respondents or 30.37 per cent (highest frequency) of the total sample has completed high school / matriculated, while the mothers' of 82 respondents or 42.93 per cent (highest frequency) of the sample are illiterate. As given in the Table, only 25 respondents or 13.09 per cent of the respondent's fathers' are illiterate, while on the contrary about 82 respondents or 42.93 per cent of their mothers' are illiterate.

Table 3.6

Distribution of respondents according to parent's educational status.

Sl. No.	Parent's Educational Status	Percent (%) students according to			
		Father's Education		Mother's Education	
		Number	%	Number	%
1	Illiterate	25	13.09	82	**42.93**
2	Completed primary school	13	6.80	21	10.99
3	Completed middle school	15	7.85	17	8.90
4	High school - not completed	23	12.04	22	11.52
5	Completed high school/matriculate	58	**30.37**	38	19.90
6	Completed intermediate / PU	19	9.95	05	2.62
7	BA / MA	38	19.90	06	3.14
	Total	191	100.00	191	100.00

The father's education and mother's education - respectively in the category of completed primary school category are 13 respondents or 6.80 per cent and 21 respondents or 10.99 per cent; in completed middle school category - it is 15 respondents or 7.85 per cent and 17 respondents or 8.90 per cent respectively; in high school not completed category - it is 23 respondents or 12.04 per cent and 22 respondents or 11.52 per cent respectively; in completed high school / matriculated category - it is 58 respondents or 30.37 and 38 respondents or 19.90 per cent respectively; in completed intermediate / PU category - it is 19 respondents or 9.95 per cent and 5 respondents or 2.62 per cent respectively; in BA / MA category - it is 38 respondents or 19.90 per cent, but on the contrary only 6 respondents or 3.14 per cent of their mothers' are graduates or post-graduates.

It is interesting to note that 60.22 per cent of the respondents' fathers are educated (matric & plus), while only 25.66 per cent of the respondents' mothers are educated. In other words, about 39.78 per cent of the fathers are uneducated while 74.34 per cent of the mothers are uneducated. And this means that there probably is no relation, no association between the respondent's level of education and the parents' education. For the total sample (191) of the respondents is constituted by the educated, right from the matriculate to the post-graduate level. Whereas on the other hand, not speaking of doing some schooling, we have 13.09 per cent and 42.93 per cent respectively of fathers and mothers who are illiterate. It can also mean the transition from an uneducated, illiterate generation to an educated, literate present generation.

Nevertheless, as observed by the number of educated unemployed in the state, education does not seem to be paying enough as it is expected. Education has failed to give a gainful employment to the educated youth, which is depicted by the prevailing problem of unemployment in our educated segment. It does not teach the student to work in the fields; rather it gives a golden dream of being a babu in an air-conditioned office, which leaves the greater majority jobless.

viii. Father's Income, Family's Income:

Income gives an insight into the economic status of the family that is instrumental in forming the external behaviour pattern of the unemployed youth in the society. (Bajpai, 1992).

Table 3.7 gives a complete idea of the father's monthly income as well as the total family's monthly income of the respondents. The monthly income has been divided into 6 income groups and has been studied on the basis of the 4 family types. The monthly income groups are a) 0-1000, b) 1000-2000, c) 2000-3000, d) 3000-4000, e) 4000-5000, and f) above 5000.

It is observed from the Table that 8.90 per cent of father's income of the educated unemployed youth come under Rs. 0-1000 income group, 2.62 per cent in Rs. 1000-2000 income group, 8.38 per cent in Rs. 2000-3000 income group, 5.33 per cent in Rs. 3000-4000 income group, 9.42 per cent in Rs. 4000-5000 income group, 43.46 per cent in Rs. above 5000 income group; while 21.99 per cent of the respondents have not specified. In the same Table, it depicts that 1.57 per cent of the total family's income of educated unemployed youth come under Rs 0-1000 income group, nil in Rs.1000-2000 income group, 1.05 per cent in Rs. 2000-3000 income group, 3.67 per cent in Rs. 3000-4000 income group, 3.67 per cent in Rs. 4000-5000 income group, 73.29 per cent in Rs. above 5000 income group; while 16.75 per cent of the respondents have not specified. It has to be noted that in all the 4 types of family, both father's monthly income and the total family's monthly income have the highest frequency in the income group - Rs. above 5000.

The Table also depicts that the percentages of family's income in all the 5 income groups excluding the income group above Rs. 5000 is minimal. Therefore it appears that most of the educated unemployed youth belong to higher income group (73.29 per cent above Rs 5000 per month). About 70.80 per cent of the family's monthly income from nuclear families is above Rs 5000. And as expected, the monthly family's income of the joint families and the extended families stands higher respectively at 75.00 per cent and 90.00 per cent in the same income group. The family's monthly income of the divorced families is also above Rs 5000 with 66.66 per cent. It means that the respondents of the sample are not from poor families, if not, from rich families. Most of the families have a stable family income to support a big family size group of 8 members (average family size = 8 as discussed in next section of the same chapter).

Many respondents who could not specify the father's income and family's income put a few questions. The reasons could be like - i) These respondents are from very low-income group where they hesitate to mention, ii) The parents may not be holding any proper job. iii) These respondents might have lost both parents and thus dependent on somebody else. iv) The family may not have stable monthly-fixed income and, therefore, difficult to calculate. v) Or the question itself might have been embarrassing to them.

ix. Type and Size of Family:

The type and size of family form the values and norms of the individual. And educated unemployed youth are no exception to this rule.

As given in the Table, for the study purpose, the families have been classified into the 4 main types, though other types of families also exist in the Naga Society. For instance, blended families are there - which consist of a husband and wife, children of previous marriages, and any children from the new marital union. However, the 4 main types of families are: a) nuclear family, b) joint family, c) extended family and, d) divorced family.

Table 3.7 above, depicts that 71.73 per cent of educated unemployed belong to nuclear families, 14.66 per cent to joint families, 10.47 per cent to extended families and 3.14 per cent belong to divorced families.

And it is obvious and understandable that most of the respondents are from nuclear families because the kinship structure of a Naga family is nuclear. A nuclear family is a unit composed of a married couple and their dependent children. The study sample also contains as many as 183 Naga respondents (or only 08 Non-Nagas) who practice monogamy i.e. one spouse at one time (few polygyny cases are also there), who are by line descent (inheritance) - patrilineal, by rules of residence - patrilocal, and by power relationships - this Naga society is patriarchal.

Table 3.7
Father's Income and Total Family's Income

Family Type	Monthly Income (Rs / Month)							Total (%)
	0-1000	1000-2000	2000-3000	3000-4000	4000-5000	Above 5000	Not Specified	
1. *Nuclear*								
a) F's/income	12 (8.76)	02 (1.46)	12 (8.76)	08 (5.84)	12 (8.76)	**60 (43.79)**	31 (22.63)	**137 (71.73)**
b) Family's income	03 (2.19)	0.00	02 (1.46)	07 (5.11)	04 (2.92)	**97 (70.80)**	24 (17.32)	
2. *Joint*								
a) F's/income	04 (14.29)	01 (3.57)	01 (3.57)	01 (3.57)	01 (3.57)	**14 (50.00)**	06 (21.43)	**28 (14.66)**
b) Family's income	0.00	0.00	0.00	0.00	02 (7.14)	**21 (75.00)**	05 (17.86)	
3. *Extended*								
a) F's/income	0.00	02 (10.00)	03 (15.00)	0.00	03 (15.00)	**07 (35.00)**	05 (25.00)	**20 (10.47)**
b) Family's income	0.00	0.00	0.00	0.00	0.00	**18 (90.00)**	02 (10.00)	

4. *Divorced*								
a) F's/income	01 (16.67)	0.00	0.00	01 (16.67)	**02 (33.32)**	**02 (33.32)**	0.00	**06 (3.14)**
b) Family's income	0.00	0.00	0.00	0.00	01 (16.67)	**04 (66.66)**	01 (16.67)	
Total F's income (Sum of a's)	17 (8.90)	05 (2.62)	16 (8.38)	10 (5.23)	18 (9.42)	**83 (43.46)**	42 (21.99)	**191 (100.00)**
Total Family's Income (Sum of b's)	03 (1.57)	0.00	02 (1.05)	07 (3.67)	07 (3.67)	**140 (73.29)**	32 (16.75)	**191 (100.00)**

Note: Mode (F's income & Total Family's income) = above 5000

Table 3.8
Family size of the respondents

Sl No	Family size	Number	%
1	1 – 3	05	2.62
2	4 – 6	56	29.32
3	7 – 9	92	**48.17**
4	10 – 12	37	19.37
5	13 – 15	01	0.52
	Total	191	100.00

Note: Mode (highest frequency) = (7 - 9) family size group.
Mean = 7.58 members.

As given in Table 3.8, the family size of the respondents has been categorized into 5 groups with three intervals each as a) 1 - 3, b) 4 - 6, c) 7 - 9, d) 10 -12, and e) 13 -15. It is observed from the Table that 2.62 per cent of the educated unemployed youth belong to 1 - 3 family size group, 29.32 per cent to 4 - 6 family size group, 48.17 per cent to 7 - 9 family size group, 19.37 per cent to 10 -12 family size group and 0.52 per cent comes from 13 -15 family size group. It also has to be noted that the highest frequency or mode is 7 - 9 family size group and the mean of the family size is 7.58 members.

An average family size of 8 members is a big family i.e. father, mother, and six children. In a Naga society, children are still accepted as a blessing. If there is any penetration of modern family planning, it has penetrated only to a small section of the society. Many families still are opposed to family planning programmes, which is further strengthened by the Christian doctrines. And the sample has revealed that about 95.81 per cent belong to Christianity.

From the economic point of view, it is not easy to maintain 8 members unless someone in the family has a proper stable job with high income. The family size is related to population and also contributes to the population growth. For that matter Nagaland state has shown the highest decade growth rate from 1991 - 2001 with 64.41 per cent growth rate. Again the high rate of unemployment and the population growth are complimentary. Therefore the state policy makers/planners in devising any policy should take both into account.

As represented by the structure, the present study contains 63.35 per cent male and 36.65 per cent female sample, where 23.04 per cent respondents are from the arts faculty, 21.99 per cent represents science faculty, 21.47 per cent from the commerce faculty, 9.95 per cent from law, 8.38 per cent from the engineering, and 7.33 per cent sample from the medicine stream. The mean age group of the sample is 24.51 years consisting pre-dominantly of unmarried educated youth. The fathers' of these respondents are mainly, either clerical workers or administrators, while the mothers are mainly housewives. The present study also contains 30.37 per cent of whose fathers' has completed high school or has matriculated, while 42.93 per cent of the mothers' are illiterate. The study reveals that the monthly income of both the father as well as the family is above Rs. 5000.The sample of the present study also has about 95 per cent Christians with 71.73 per cent belonging to nuclear families, while the mean of the family size is 7.58 members.

4

Aspirations, Preferences and Expectations

The previous chapter discusses the socio-economic background, i.e. the personal characteristics of the respondents. Now, in this chapter, it discusses about the aspirations of the educated job seekers, which are reflected in their preferences for particular jobs. The chapter discusses about the job expectations of the educated unemployed youth in proportion with their preferences for occupations. This chapter also discusses about the criteria for satisfactory jobs, and the preferences on job locations.

i. Aspirations:

When young men find they have to wait for years to get employment and then to content themselves with petty jobs, they feel greatly upset. The youth seek a stable life but cannot secure it; they are hungry for opportunities, recognition and status. They feel that instead of sympathy and consideration, they get general denunciation and condemnation. They have to frequently bear derogatory remarks against the whole lot of youth. (Bajpai, 1992). The youth of today, who are the nation builders of tomorrow complain of mounting frustration, and are largely a discontented lot. Their vast energies and labour force, intelligence and knowledge are being wasted and remains untapped.

Any solution to the problem of the educated unemployed would require information on the aspirations of the unemployed and the availability of the job opportunities in its particular situation. Aspirations of job seekers, of the educated unemployed youth are reflected in their preferences and desires for particular jobs.

Indian youth tend to nurture materialistic aspirations like their Western counterparts. Hardly anyone wants to be a Gandhi or a Nehru, Buddha or Mahavira, Rama or Krishna; rather most of them want just a secure and prosperous life. It is true that in the contemporary materialistic society money and material resources form the core of human aspirations. Money gives power over men and materials (Bajpai, 1992). The present study reveals that this is a relevant reference with the educated unemployed youth of Nagaland State. As the study presents the jobs most desired by the unemployed are in the organized sector of the economy, i.e. government jobs, for the simple reasons that government jobs promised stability and security of tenure with assured levels of wages and salaries along with guaranteed retirement benefits. Moreover, the society also attaches glamour, prestige status and importance to the government jobs. At the same time, the educated youth are under pressure from their respective parents and relatives who not only have high expectations but also want their educated wards to secure government jobs. Interestingly, it is a reflection of Cooley's theory of 'looking glass self', which accordingly is, in the course of socialization, individual develops 'self' and 'social consciousness' simultaneously and looks his image in the society. And since society pays high regard for government jobs, every youth aspires for government jobs than any other.

The present study sample reveals that 67.01 per cent preferred government jobs to self-employed jobs (26.18 per cent) and private jobs (6.81 per cent). It therefore indicates that most educated unemployed youth does not like the hard work, but they (67.01 per cent) want sedentary jobs. The educated first preferred choice is relatively for white-collar jobs. They seem to be inclined towards the desk job.

However, at the same time, in case of no other alternative the educated youth are ready for even manual jobs. It has been depicted that 83.25 per cent are ready for manual jobs in case of no other alternative. It could be therefore concluded here that, though the youth prefers government jobs, yet the final aspiration is found to consist in getting any job in order to earn a livelihood.

The present study also depicts that though 53.93 per cent of the educated youth are satisfied with their education and faculty, yet 54.45 per cent are not satisfied with their various degrees, qualifications and trainings. It therefore highlights that though the majority of the respondents are satisfied with their education faculty, they are not satisfied with their degrees and qualifications. They are not satisfied with the trainings. May be they are not satisfied with the manner the training is imparted. Or may be they are totally frustrated with their respective degrees, qualifications for it could not help them in getting any job. While 71.73 per cent of the educated unemployed youth are not sure of getting a satisfactory job, at least 22.51 per cent are hopeful to get a satisfactory job.

ii. Motivations for Seeking Education:

Like students throughout the world, Indian students seek education for a number of reasons. The motivations might well be simultaneously mundane, noble and realistic (Dhar, 1976). For some educated youth, a respective degree ensures respect and status in the community, particularly when opportunities are less or in short supply. For others, the main purpose is to achieve a competitive edge in the job market. While some pursue their studies as being desired by parents and relatives; yet some others do, for not getting any jobs. Some others are motivated by genuine love for learning.

As given in Tables 4.1 and 4.2, the educated unemployed youth are asked to indicate and rank the most important and the second most important reasons that prompted them to seek college education or university education or technical education. An analysis of their responses (Table 4.1) indicated that 68.59 per cent ranked to "acquire more knowledge" as the most important reason for seeking education; 15.71 per cent ranked "prospect of a higher paying job"; 12.04 per cent ranked "respect and status in the community"; 2.62 per cent ranked "could not get a job"; and 0.52 per cent ranked "desired by parents and relatives" as the most important reason that has motivated them for education. Therefore, the desire to "acquire more knowledge" emerged as the primary reason for the respondents to seek further education after matriculation. In other words, the majority of the respondents are motivated by genuine love for learning. The opportunity afforded by the college or university for acquiring more knowledge became saliently the major motivating factor for these respondents. And a calculated 39.79 per cent (highest percentage) of the responses marked "respect and status in the community" as the second most important reason for seeking education. It indicates that the community and to gain community respect influences the choice of many students. The respondents in other words, go for higher education because it enables them to have respect and better status above others in the community. It also has to be noted that 01 respondent has a concern for society, which motivates him to seek more education.

Table 4.1
Reasons for seeking College/University/Technical Education

Sl No	Reasons	Students Ranking it (In %ages) i Most Important	ii Second most Important
i	Respect and status in the community	12.04	39.79
ii	Prospect of a higher paying job	15.71	24.08
iii	Desired by parents / relatives	0.52	12.57
iv	Acquire more knowledge	**68.59**	16.75
v	Could not get a job	2.62	6.81

Note: 1 respondent (0.52) remarked - concern for society - as the most important reason).

The faculty-wise distribution of the respondents' ranking the various factors as the most important reason for seeking college education or university education or technical education is provided in Table 4.2 given below.

Table 4.2
Faculty-wise distribution of Respondents (Educated Unemployed Youth)
Ranking the various factors as the most important

Sl No.	Faculty	Percent (%) students ranking the factors as the most important				
		more knowledge	community respect	no job after high school	higher paying job	parental desire
1	Arts (44)	**70.45**	9.09	6.82	13.64	0.00
2	Science (42)	**73.81**	9.52	0.00	14.29	2.38
3	Commerce (41)	**68.29**	14.63	2.45	14.63	0.00
4	Engineering (16)	**50.00**	0.00	0.00	**50.00**	0.00
5	Medicine (14)	**57.14**	21.43	0.00	14.29	7.14
6	Law (19)	**84.21**	5.26	0.00	10.53	0.00
	All Faculties (176)	**69.32**	10.23	2.27	17.04	1.14

Note: Total = 191 - 15 (matriculates) = 176.

As depicted in the Table (Table 4.2), in all the faculties, the highest percentage of responses marked as the most important reason is to "acquire more knowledge" - arts (70.45), science (73.81), commerce (68.29), engineering (50.00), medicine (57.14) and law (84.21). It should be noted that 50.00 per cent each of the educated unemployed youth coming from the engineering faculty have marked to "acquire more knowledge" and "prospect of a higher paying job" as the most important reason for doing engineering degree. And it is obvious because majority of the respondents believed that the engineering job is the best job to earn money. Therefore, many brilliant students have joined this technical institution with a prospect of being paid higher in getting a job. The respondents from the arts, science, commerce and law faculty expects that with higher degrees and qualifications, they would be paid better in getting a job. Again, it is obvious that 21.43 per cent from the medicine category has been motivated to study medicine in order to gain community respect and status.

Table 4.3

Reasons for seeking college or university or technical education according to the occupational status of the father

Father's occupational status	Influencing factors ranked as first in importance (in percentages).					
	I Respect and status in the community	II Prospect of a higher paying job	III Desired by parents and relatives	iV To acquire more knowledge	V Could not get a job	VI Total
Professional/Technical (17)	02 (1.05)	03 (1.57)	0.00	12 (6.28)	0.00	17 (8.90)
Administrative/Executive (42)	06 (3.14)	06 (3.14)	0.00	30(15.71)	0.00	42(21.99)
Clerical workers (49)	05 (2.62)	04 (2.09)	0.00	38(19.90)	02(1.05)	49(25.65)
Sales Workers/Business (20)	04 (2.09)	07 (3.66)	01(0.52)	07 (3.66)	01(0.52)	20(1.47)
Farmers/Craftsmen (25)	02 (1.05)	07 (3.66)	0.00	15 (7.85)	01(0.52)	25(13.09)
Others (38)	04 (2.09)	03 (1.57)	0.00	29(15.18)	01(0.52)	37+1=38 (19.90)
Total	23(12.04)	30(15.71)	01(0.52)	**131(64.59)**	05(2.62)	191(100.00)

Note: In others 1 respondent (0.52) remarked - concern for society- as the most important reason.

One would assume that the youth motivations would vary with differences in the socio-economic status of the family, the positional and occupational status differences of the father. Those with little status in the community are likely to seek higher education / degrees for gaining communal respect, while those whose families enjoying higher status will use higher education for further enhancing their economic position. However, the data (Table 4.3) is not conclusive on this assumption.

As depicted in the Table above, the desire to acquire more knowledge emerged as the main reason for all occupational groups, followed by the prospects of a higher paying job that a degree opens for its holder. And gaining community respect through attainment of higher qualification follows this. However, gaining community respect does not seem to influence the choice of many students as is expected. Education is considered a major instrument for social mobility, to gain respect and status in the community, but the data indicates that there are other more important reasons in seeking education. The data indicates for all occupational groups, there is only 01 respondent who pursues education by the motivation of parents and relatives. It means the students are not seeking education as desired by parents and relatives, but in order to acquire more knowledge, in order to achieve a competitive edge in the job market.

Again, the data in Table 4.4 reveals that the difference in father's income and total family's income also do not affect the relative importance of the factors. The desire to acquire more knowledge emerged as the primary reason for all income groups as shown in the Table. It has to be noted that the majority of the respondents in the sample are from higher income groups i.e. above Rs. 5000 (monthly). And this fact suggests that they are already enjoying a higher status in their communities and the higher education does not particularly enhance it for them. The data in the Table reveals that even the respondents from lower income groups, from poor families marks "acquiring more knowledge" as the primary motivation and not having any other reason. To acquire more knowledge thus emerged as the main motivation irrespective of being poor or rich.

iii. Choice of Faculties:

In addition to studying the motivations for college education or university education or technical education, the respondent youths' are also asked to make a choice of the faculty in which he wishes to study. One would assume that the choice of faculty is determined substantially by factors such as - the socio-economic status of the family, examination performances, parental wishes, possibilities of remunerative employment, status associated with different fields of study, and failure to get admitted to another faculty, etc.

The study shows a general satisfaction among the respondent youth about their current choice of faculties. In response to the question, "Are you satisfied with your education and faculty?" about 53.93 per cent of the educated unemployed respondents indicated yes, while 46.07 per cent indicated no in answering the question.

Table 4.5 depicts a clear picture of the educated unemployed youth preferences for faculties. This Table is drawn in response to the question, "If you are given a choice to study again, which study stream/faculty would you prefer?" As shown in the Table, out of the total 44 arts respondents, 59.09 per cent prefers its own field, i.e. arts; 15.91 per cent prefers to study law; 11.36 per cent prefers science; 9.09 per cent prefers to study commerce; 4.55 per cent prefers to study medicine; while no respondent in this category prefers for engineering. Among the total 42 science respondents, again 50.00 per cent prefers its own field; 26.19 per cent prefers to study medicine; 11.91 per cent prefers commerce; 7.14 per cent prefers arts; 2.38 per cent engineering; another 2.38 per cent prefers to study computer; while no respondent from the science category prefers to study law. In the commerce category, out of the total 41 respondents, 70.73 per cent prefers to study commerce still; 12.19 per cent law; 7.32 per cent engineering; 4.88 per cent arts; another 4.88 per cent medicine; while no respondent prefers to study science. Out of the total 19 law respondents, 73.68 per cent prefers to study law again; 10.53 per cent engineering; another 10.53 per cent medicine; 5.26 per cent commerce; while no one from this category prefers for arts and science. In the engineering group, out of the total 16 respondents, 75.00 percent prefers its own field; 18.17 per cent commerce; 6.25 per cent medicine; while no respondent from

Table 4.4

Reasons for seeking college or university or technical education according to father's monthly income and total family's income.

Father's income / Total Family's income (In Rs.)	Percentage of ranking the factor as the most important				
	i Respect and status in the community	ii Prospect of a higher paying job	iii Desired by parents and relatives	iv To acquire more knowledge	v Could not get a job
1. *0 - 1000*					
a) **Father's income (17)**	01 (0.52)	04 (2.09)	0.00	11 (5.76)	01 (0.52)
b) **T. family's income (03)**	01 (0.52)	0.00	0.00	02 (1.05)	0.00
2. *1000 - 2000*					
a) **Father's income (05)**	0.00	0.00	0.00	05 (2.62)	0.00
b) **T. family's income (00)**	0.00	0.00	0.00	0.00	0.00
3. *2000 - 3000*					
a) **Father's income (16)**	0.00	04 (2.09)	0.00	11 (5.76)	01 (0.52)
b) **T. family's income (02)**	0.00	0.00	0.00	02 (1.05)	0.00

4. *3000 - 4000*					
a) Father's income (10)	02 (1.05)	03 (1.57)	0.00	05 (2.62)	0.00
b) T. family's income (07)	02 (1.05)	0.00	0.00	03 (1.57)	02 (1.05)
5. *4000 - 5000*					
a) Father's income (18)	05 (2.62)	02 (1.05)	0.00	10 (5.24)	01 (0.52)
b) T. family's income (07)	03 (1.57)	02 (1.05)	0.00	01 (0.52)	01 (0.52)
6. *Above 5000*					
a) Father's income (83)	11 (5.76)	15 (7.85)	01 (0.52)	55 (28.79)	01 (0.52)
b) T. family's income (140)	15 (7.85)	23(12.04)	01 (0.52)	99 (51.83)	02 (1.05)

Note: Not specified - i) Father's income= 42 (21.99), ii) Total family's income = 32 (16.75).

Table 4.5
Educated Unemployed Youth's preferences for faculties.

Sl No	Faculty	Percent (%) students indicating preferences for.							
		i Own field	ii Arts	iii Science	iv Commerce	v Law	vi Engineering	vii Medicine	viii Any other
1	Arts (44)	**59.09**	-	11.36	9.09	15.91	0.0	04.55	0.00
2	Science (42)	**50.00**	7.14	-	11.91	0.00	2.38	26.19	2.38
3	Commerce (41)	**70.73**	4.88	0.00	-	12.19	7.32	4.88	0.00
4	Law (19)	**73.68**	0.00	0.00	5.26	-	10.53	10.53	0.00
5	Engineering (16)	**75.00**	0.00	0.00	18.75	0.00	-	6.25	0.00
6	Medicine (14)	**50.00**	28.75	0.00	14.29	0.00	0.00	-	7.14

[Note: In (vii) any other - 2 respondents preferred to study Computers].

this category prefers to study arts, science and law. In the medicine faculty, out of the total 14 respondents, 50.00 per cent prefers its own field; 28.75 per cent prefers to study arts; 14.29 per cent commerce; 7.14 per cent prefers for studying computers; while no respondent from this group prefers to study science, law and engineering if they are given a chance to study again.

In their study, T.N. Dhar, A.S. Ilchman & W.F. Ilchman finds out that engineering and medicine emerged as the most preferred faculties, which are noted for better and more remunerative employment opportunities. (Dhar, 1976). In contrast, the present study shows that the respondents of the different faculty groups prefer their own field. In other words, they are satisfied with their education and faculty. However, this does not compliment 46.07 per cent who has indicated that they are not satisfied with their education and faculty. Therefore, the responses of these two inter-related questions have resulted into contradiction. Because on one hand, the respondents (46.07 per cent) answered they are not satisfied with their education and faculty, and on the other hand, these respondents (63.08 per cent) prefers their own faculty if they are given a chance to study again.

iv. Job Preferences and Job Expectations:

The occupational choices of the educated youths' are influenced by a variety of factors: i) the economic returns associated with a job, ii) the social prestige that it carries, iii) the type of education and exercise and iv) security and future prospects - considered suitable to it (Dhar, 1976).

As given in Table 4.6, the respondents are asked to rank in order of importance, the four factors, which influence the occupational choices most. About 41.88 per cent of the respondents marked the type of education and training as the most influential factor. About 35.08 per cent of the respondents marked the economic returns associated with a job as the second choice. And about 41.88 per cent and 34.03 per cent of the respondents has marked the social prestige that it carries as the third and the fourth preferences respectively. It is obvious that the most influential factor for occupational choices is the type of education and training the respective educated youth has. For the job seeker also should know what kind of job he is qualified and accordingly looks for it. For instance, an arts graduate cannot apply for a medical doctor, but is meant for those who are qualified as MBBS or MD. Likewise, a medical doctor with his medical degree cannot teach in Arts College. In other words, a realistic appraisal of suitability seems to lead the educated youth to choose and expect occupations more in line with their training, whether they prefer them or not. Again, it has to be noted that all the four factors discussed above are complimentary and no single factor alone solely influences the unemployed youth for choosing his/her occupation. However, on the basis of the responses as given in the Table, we can arrange the preferences in order of importance as - type of education and training, security and future prospects, economic returns associated with a job and lastly social prestige that it carries as the least influential factor of all.

Table 4.6
Influential Factors for Occupational Choices.

	Factors	Preferences			
		1st	2nd	3rd	4th
i	Economic returns associated with a job	29(15.18)	**67(35.08)**	52(27.22)	41(21.47)
ii	Social prestige that it carries	16(8.38)	28(14.66)	**80(41.88)**	**65(34.03)**
iii	Type of education and training	**80(41.88)**	34(17.80)	23(12.05)	52(27.22)
iv	Security and future prospects	64(33.51)	**60(31.41)**	34(17.80)	31(16.23)

[**Note:** unanswered = 02 (1.05)].

One may assume that, what the educated unemployed youth prefers may not necessarily be the vocation he chooses. However, their preferences do have substantial influence on occupational choice, especially when educational choices have been made based on future occupational goals. It is obligatory to make a distinction between the occupations the educated youth prefer and the occupations that they expect to get. Dhar, in his study of the college and university students showed little discrepancy between preferences and expectations. (Dhar, 1976). On the other hand, Foster found a great discrepancy between the occupational preferences and the occupational expectations of Ghana school students. (Foster, 1963). The present study of the educated unemployed youth also showed a great discrepancy between the occupational preferences and the occupational expectations.

There is no correspondence at all between the proportions indicating preference for occupations and those indicating the occupations that the educated youth expect to get. The difference between the two ranges from a low of -33.51 percent and a high of +12.04 percent. For instance, 48.69 per cent of the educated unemployed youth preferred to be administrative official but only 15.18 per cent expected to get it resulting in a wide discrepancy of -33.51 per cent. Again, only 6.28 per cent of the educated youth preferred to salesman/business job, but 18.32 per cent of the youth are expecting to get it showing a discrepancy gap of +12.04 per cent.

The study further reveals that high administrative positions emerged to be very attractive. Perhaps the preference for this occupation is strongly influenced by the perception of the change in the economic and social position. The occupation - high administrative official have become scarce and the competition to this position even stiffer. Consequently, this high administrative job acquires better economic position, higher status, higher prestige and glamour than before. On the other hand, some occupations like secondary school teacher, law and clerkship, etc. which have been perceived to have declined in economic and social position, are not generally preferred even by those whose qualifications would make them more suitable for them.

It is to be noted that "to acquire more knowledge" and preferring for administrative jobs rather than academic jobs in occupation are in itself contradictory. Moreover, the salary of administrative officials and university/college teachers is more or less at par.

Table 4. 7
Occupational Preferences and Expectations of Educated Unemployed Youth

Sl No.	Occupations	Proportion of Students i Preferring	Proportion of Students ii Expecting	Difference between Preference (i) & Expectation (ii).
1	Administrative Official	48.69	15.18	- **33.51**
2	University Teacher	5.76	12.04	+ 6.28
3	Secondary School Teacher	0.00	8.38	+ 8.38
4	Higher Research	5.76	3.14	- 2.62
5	Legal (Law) Practitioner	1.57	4.19	+ 2.62
6	Engineer	5.76	4.71	- 1.05
7	Physician/Surgeon	9.95	6.81	- 3.14
8	Salesman/Business	6.28	18.32	+ **12.04**
9	Contractors & Suppliers	2.09	0.52	- 1.57
10	Clerk	0.00	6.28	+ 6.28
11	Farmer	1.57	1.57	0.00
12	Politician/Political Agent	0.52	4.19	+ 3.67
13	Editor/Journalist	2.09	1.57	- 0.52
14	Military/Police	6.81	7.85	+ 1.04
15	Others	3.14	5.24	+ 2.10
	Total	100.00	100.00	
	Number	191	191	

The present study also tries to understand the willingness / unwillingness of the educated unemployed youth (respondents) to work in the rural areas / urban areas. The respondents are asked to indicate their preferences when it comes to higher pay or lower pay, work that is more interesting or less interesting, more job security or less job security, nearer home or distant location. They are asked to indicate their preferences for two jobs, which are similar to each other in all but two respects.

Table 4.8
Educated unemployed youth preferences for jobs / locations

Sl No	Job Characteristics	Proportions a / b
1	Higher pay with less interesting work / Lower pay with more interesting work.	33.51 / 66.49
2	Higher pay with less job security / Lower pay with more job security.	34.03 / 65.97
3	More interesting work in distant location / Less interesting work nearer home	69.63 / 30.37
4	Nearer home with lower pay / Distant location with more pay.	26.18 / 73.82
5	Urban location with lower pay / Rural area with higher pay.	53.93 / 46.07
6	Nearer home in rural area / Distant but in an urban area.	47.64 / 52.36

As indicated in the Table, the data shows that the jobs, which offered scope for interesting work and security, are preferred even when they offered fewer monetary rewards. The location of the job is not the primary consideration, especially when higher salary and work that is more interesting are the factors. In such a case the disincentives are associated with the job rather than where it is located. According to the study, given interesting work and job security, work in rural areas is not particularly disliked by the educated unemployed youth. Again, the preferences for distant urban locations is slightly greater that rural areas nearer home. In other words, when the choice of urban and rural is offered, majority of the respondents preferred urban areas though it would have been far from home. May be, the primary option to urban areas is attributed to the expectations that are created among students in urban-based universities. This attitude might be because of the livelihood that works in the rural areas are less stimulating professionally, immobile and dull, etc.

v. Criteria for Satisfactory Jobs:

In this section, the educated unemployed youth are studied as to how they perceive acquiring a satisfactory job. In response to the question, "Will you get a satisfactory job?" - about 71.73 per cent of the respondent youth are not sure of getting a satisfactory job. However, the study reveals that about 22.51 per cent are confident of getting a satisfactory job.

From the point of view of manpower planning, how the youth perceive acquiring a job is nearly as important as the job that they might choose. As shown in Table 4.9, the educated unemployed youth are asked to rank, in order of importance, the factors that are important in getting a satisfactory job. And the study reveals that education (51.83 per cent) is regarded as the most important factor for obtaining satisfactory jobs while hard work (34.03 per cent) is regarded as the second most important criteria for satisfactory jobs.

Table 4.9

Factors responsible/important for getting a satisfactory job.

Sl No	Factors	Proportions ranking it as i The most important	ii The second most important
1	Education	**51.83**	12.04
2	Hard work	27.23	**34.03**
3	Ability	9.42	27.23
4	Personal contacts	0.00	2.10
5	Influential friends & contacts	0.52	1.05
6	Recommendations from important persons (politicians, govt. officials)	5.76	10.47
7	Luck	3.67	6.28
8	Bribery	1.05	6.28
9	Others	0.52	0.52

The factors have been categorized into two - i) "achievement oriented" and ii) "tradition oriented" (Dhar, 1976). The first three factors from the Table - education, hard work, and ability can easily fall into the achievement-oriented category, but placing of some of the other criteria presents problems. Using this rough scale we find that about 88.48 per cent of the educated unemployed youth regard achievement criteria to be the most important factor for satisfactory jobs; 6.28 per cent regard - personal contacts, influential friends, and recommendations of important persons to be the most crucial factor; while 4.72 per cent of the educated youth felt that bribery and luck are helpful to get a satisfactory job. The study indicates that more than fourth/fifth of the educated unemployed youth perceives achievement criteria as the primary factor for acquiring a job. Perhaps these respondents have fewer sources or influences, that they are just likely to show greater reliance on education, hard work, and ability. It is usual for personal contacts and recommendations to play a crucial part in job seeking. Again, it is obvious that some respondents rely on bribery as the most important factor to get satisfactory jobs because bribery prevails in the state. These respondents relying on bribery to get a job possibly must be from rich backgrounds and either being totally frustrated or lazy to work hard and compete with others.

Thus to conclude, the aspirations of the educated unemployed youth are reflected in their preferences and desires for particular jobs. The unemployed wants a secure, stable and prosperous job. As discussed, the jobs most desired by the unemployed are the government jobs that promises stability and security of tenure with assured levels of wages and salaries along with guaranteed retirement benefits. Most educated job seekers do not like the hard work, but they want sedentary jobs and are inclined towards the desk job. Their first preferred choice is relatively for white-collar jobs. However, majority of them are ready for even manual jobs in case of no other alternative. Therefore, though the unemployed educated youth prefer government jobs, yet the final aspiration is found to consist in getting any job in order to earn a livelihood.

The desire to acquire more knowledge emerged as the primary reason for seeking education in all the faculties, for all occupational groups and for all income groups. And the youth are satisfied with their education and faculty. The educated respondents of the different faculty groups prefer their own field of study. There is a great discrepancy between the occupational preferences and the occupational expectations. In other words, there is no correspondence between the proportions indicating preferences for occupations and those indicating the occupations that the educated youth expect to get. Again, as discussed the location of job is not the primary consideration for preferences when there is scope for interesting work, security and higher salary. Yet, preferences for urban locations are slightly greater than rural areas. Lastly, the educated unemployed youth regard achievement criteria (education, hard work, and ability) to be the most important factor for acquiring satisfactory jobs.

5

Employment Opportunities

The previous chapter discusses the aspirations of the educated youth, their preferences and desires for particular jobs. The present chapter will discuss about the literacy growth and the job/occupational structure in the state. And in relation it will discuss the perspectives of the job market and the available job opportunities. It will also discuss the frequency of job attempts by the educated unemployed youth and extent of their concern regarding unemployment.

Manpower planning aims essentially at striking a balance between the supply of workers and the demand for their services. In the case of educated manpower, the aim is to regulate the outflow from, and consequently the flow into the educational institutions in relation to the requirements of trained manpower for the economy. (Dhar, 1976). It is imperative to know the state government policy for manpower planning; whether it is a successful plan or not; whether it is balanced between supply and demand, outflow and inflow. It is imperative to study:

a) The literacy growth rate and the exact job structure in the state.

b) The existing state of the information that the educated unemployed have about the employment market.

c) The extent to which the educated are concerned with their occupational futures.

d) The perceptions of the employment situation like - the varying incidence of unemployment, the increase/decrease in availability of jobs, etc.

Now the state picture as already discussed in Chapter II, is that, one could see the increasing trend of educated youth, the continuous bulging out of students in schools and colleges, the rapid growth rate of literacy. These are the supply of workers. They remain as educated unemployed, for they are not fitted into the employment scenario. The number of educated persons has grown very fast compared to the expansion of the job opportunities. The future of the educated unemployed is expected to be very bleak in view of the shrinking employment opportunities, particularly in the organized sector. Therefore, if there is no balance between the number of students produced and the number of jobs available; we simply see the expansion of unemployment, the expansion of educated unemployment as seen in Chapter 2. The outflow and the inflow of the state has to be balanced.

i. Literacy Growth:

The literacy rate has steadily increased since the last six decades. Table 5.1 indicates the literacy growth in Nagaland since 1951 to 2001.

Table 5.1
Literacy Growth in Nagaland (1951 - 2001) (6 decades).

Year (Census)	Persons	Males	Females
1951	10.52	15.18	5.75
1961	21.95	29.22	14.02
1971	33.78	42.57	23.38
1981	50.28	58.58	40.39
1991	61.65	67.62	54.75
2001	67.11	71.77	61.92

Note: Literacy rates for 1951, 1961 and 1971 relate to the population-aged 5 years and above. The rates for the years 1981 to 2001 relate to the population-aged 7 years and above.

Source: Census Department, Kohima.

It could be seen from Table 5.1 that the literacy rate in Nagaland has increased gradually from 10.52 in 1951 to 67.11 in 2001. The percentage of literate men and women to the total respective population have also steadily increased from 15.18 in 1951 to 71.77 in 2001 in the case of men and 5.75 in 1951 to 61.92 in 2001 in the case of women. The population growth, the literacy growth, the job structure and the growth of employment correspond to the growth of unemployment in the state. And the government policy in curbing the problem of unemployment among the educated youth is related and can be closely examined based on these factors. The increased literate data discussed above depicts increased population of educated in the state in the last 6 decades. Accordingly, this data perhaps demands on the policy makers and planners to create more jobs suitable for the educated population based on its proportion.

ii. Job / Occupational Structure in the State:

The Census Department has classified the entire population into three main occupational categories: 1) Main Workers, 2) Marginal Workers and 3) Non-Workers.

1. Main Workers

Main Workers are those who have worked for the major part of the year preceding the date of enumeration i.e. those who are engaged in any economically productive activity for 183 days or six months or more during the year.

Main Workers are further classified into four broad industrial categories:

a) *Cultivators*: A person is considered as a cultivator if he or she is engaged either as employer, single worker or family worker in cultivation of land owned or held from the government or held from private persons or institutions for payment in money, kind or share of crop. Cultivation include supervision or direction of cultivation.

b) *Agricultural Labourers*: A person who works in another person's land for wages in cash, kind or share of crop is regarded as an agricultural labourer. Such a person has no risk in cultivation but merely works in another person's land for wages. An agricultural labourer has no right of lease or contract on land on which he works.

c) *Household Industry*: Household industry is defined as an industry by the head of the household himself/herself or by the members of the household at home or within the village in rural areas, and only within the precincts of the house where the household lives in urban areas.

A household industry is one that is engaged in production, processing, servicing, repairing or making and selling of goods.

d) *Other Workers*: All those who work in any field of economic activity other than cultivation, agricultural labour, or household industries are 'other workers'. The types of workers that came under this category include factory workers, plantation workers, those in trade, commerce, business, transport, mining, construction, political or social work, all government servants, municipal employees, teachers, priests, entertainment artists, etc.

2. Marginal Workers

Marginal workers are those who work any time at all in the year preceding the enumeration but did not work for a major part of the year i.e. those who work for less than 183 days or six months.

3. Non-Workers

If an individual has not worked at all during the last, he or she is treated as a non-worker. Non-workers included:

a) those attending to household duties at home;

b) students;

c) dependents;

d) retired persons or rentiers;

e) beggars,

f) inmates of institutions; and

g) other non-workers - which includes educated unemployed youth.

In view of the job opportunities and job expectations of the educated unemployed, it is relevant to examine the existing job / occupational structure in the state. The economic activity of the entire population has been classified into the following categories by the Census Department as shown in the table (Table 5.2).

As given in Table 5.2, the total population is classified into main workers, marginal workers and non-workers. In 1981, the total main workers is 368,321 which constitutes 47.53 per cent of the total population; there are 5,433 marginal workers constituting only 7.02 per cent; there are 401,176 non-workers which constitutes about 51.77 per cent of the total population (i.e. 774,930). In 1991, the proportion of the main workers is 42.29 per cent (511,497); the marginal workers are 0.39 per cent (4,740); and the non-workers are 57.32 per cent (693,309). In 2001, the proportion of the main workers has further decreased to 35.63 per cent (708,455); the marginal workers have gone up again to 7.12 per cent (141,527); and the proportion of the non-workers is 57.26 per cent (1,138,654). The non-workers, who are 401,176 in 1981, have increased to 1,138,654 in 2001 at an increased percentage of 183.83 per cent (i.e. in 2 decades).

The category - main workers is further classified into four broad industrial categories as shown in the same Table: a) cultivators, b) agricultural labourers, c) household industry and d) other workers. The proportion of cultivators to main workers in 1981 is as high as 72.29 per cent, which is also the record highest in India. In 1991 it is 72.65 per cent while break-up of main workers for 2001 is not ready at the time of data collection. The proportion of agricultural labourers, household industry, and other workers respectively in 1981 is 0.81 per cent, 0.40 per cent and 26.51 per cent; while in 1991 it is 1.41 per cent, 0.39 per cent and 25.55 per cent respectively.

From the point of view of absorption of the educated unemployed, it is necessary to understand the growth of employment. It is essential to understand the growth of main workers, the % expansion of main workers. As given in Table 5.3, the total expansion of main workers during 1981-1991 has been found to be slow, being only 38.87 per cent, which turns out to be a bare 3.89 per

Table 5.2

Job / Occupational Structure in the State (Nagaland).

Year	Total Main Workers					Marginal Workers	Non-Workers	Total Population
	i	ii	iii	iv	Total			
1981	266,241	2,979	1,461	97,640	368,321	5,433	401,176	774,930
1991	371,597	7,233	1,991	130,676	511,497	4,740	693,309	1,209,546
2001	-	-	-		708,455	141,527	1,138,654	1,988,636

Note I i) Cultivators, ii) Agricultural labourers, iii) Household industry, iv) Other workers.
Note II 2001 Census - data provisional and break-up of main workers - not ready at the time of data collection.
Source : Census Department, Kohima.

Table 5.3
Growth of Main Workers (20 years).

Year	Total Main Workers	% Expansion of Main Workers
1981	215,904 (M) + 152,417 (F) = 368,321	% Expansion of Main Workers from 1981 - 1991 = 38.87 %%
1991	299,437 (M) + 212,060 (F) = 511,497	%Yearly Expansion = 3.89 %
2001	424,236 (M) + 284,219 (F) = 708,455	% Expansion of Main Workers from 1991 -2001 = 38.51 % % Yearly Expansion = 3.85 %

(M = male, F = female)
Note: 2001 Census data - provisional.
Source: Census Department, Kohima.

cent per annum. The total expansion of main workers during 1991-2001 has shown similar slow growth, i.e. 38.51 per cent turning out to be a bare 3.85 per cent per annum.

On the other hand, the decadal population growth during 1981-1991, which is 56.08 per cent, has increased to 64.41 per cent in 1991-2000 that also recorded the highest decadal growth rate in India. We could see the decreasing trend of the proportion of main workers to total population, which in 1981 is 47.52 per cent, decreased to 42.29 per cent in 1991, and further, decreased to 35.63 per cent in 2001.

Again as discussed above, the maximum concentration of main workers are cultivators, i.e. 72.29 per cent (as of 1981) and 72.65 per cent (as of 1991). Now the educated unemployed with their degrees would surely not opt for cultivation as discussed in Chapter IV. The jobs most desired by this educated unemployed are in the organized sector of the economy, which includes public sector jobs and private sector jobs. [Public sector employment can be divided into a) central government, b) state government, c) quasi/semi government and, d) local government]. These educated youth aspire for government jobs for it promises stability and security of tenure with assured level of wages and salaries along with guaranteed retirement benefits.

The situation will worsen if there is to be any negative growth of employment in the government departments. The picture can be supplemented by the closing down of few small industries the state has such as like Tuli Paper Mill, Dimapur Sugar Mill, etc. The state government has also come up with a new policy in the wake of the emerging fiscal crisis to downsize the employed population. The seriousness of the job problem is also clearly visible taking for instance where more than 3000 candidates fight every year for few jobs conducted by the Nagaland Public Service Commission (NPSC). Therefore considering all these situations, the employment scenario does not look healthy but is gloomy for the rapidly expanding educated youth in the state.

iii. Extent of Concern:

To study the period of unemployment of the educated youth,

a question "How long have you remained unemployed?" is asked to the respondents.

Table 5.4
Period of Unemployment.

Sl No	Period in Years	Number (%)
1	0 – 1	26 (13.61)
2	1 – 2	27 (14.14)
3	2 – 3	**35 (18.32)**
4	3 – 4	25 (13.09)
5	4 – 5	15 (7.85)
6	5 – 6	14 (7.33)

Note: **Not mentioned** = **49 (25.66)**
Mode period = (2 - 3) years.
Mean = 2.63 years.

In response to the question as depicted in Table 5.4, 13.61 per cent of the educated unemployed youth has indicated that they have remained unemployed for a period of (0 - 1) years, about 14.14 per cent indicated (1 - 2) years as the unemployment period, 18.32 per cent has indicated (2 - 3) years as the period of unemployment, 13.09 per cent has indicated (3 - 4) years, 7.85 per cent has indicated (4 - 5) years, while 7.33 per cent has indicated (5 - 6) years as the period of unemployment. The mode period for unemployment is (2 - 3) years and the mean period of unemployment is 2.63 years. The average respondents of the sample have remained unemployed without any job for 3 years. In other words, these educated youth have been unsuccessfully searching remunerative jobs to earn their livelihood. The study also reveals that 15.18 per cent of the sample has remained unemployed for more than 4 years in spite of their efforts to acquire a job. Moreover, to remain unemployed for so many years depending upon the other family members for all their needs is surely frustrating. A frustrated man will be diseased which affects the family, the society and affects the nation at large. It has to be noted that 25.66 per cent of the respondents have not mentioned the period of their unemployment. Perhaps it could be possible that they have remained unemployed without any job for more than 6 years, since the classificatory period extends only up to 6 years.

The study reveals that about 93.19 per cent of the educated unemployed youth are well aware of the increasing trend of educated unemployment. In relation to the study of the unemployment period, another question "Whom do you blame most for not getting a job?" is asked with four choices: i) self ii) your education iii) family and iv) government. Of which, more than one-half i.e. 54.45 per cent has blamed 'the government' most for not getting a job; though at the same time about 87.44 per cent of the educated unemployed youth indicates that the government won't be able to employ all of them. No doubt the government cannot generate employment for every educated person; yet these majority respondents expects the government to do better. The educated unemployed respondents blame the government most for not getting a job because the appointment is biased in favour of the rich and the bureaucrats to various jobs. Corruption and favouritism in the process of selection is unanimously accepted by the unemployed youth. Generally presenting, 30.37 per cent of the respondents regard themselves guilty for unemployment, 13.09 per cent to the education system, 0.52 per cent to the family and 54.45 per cent blame the government guilty for unemployment.

As given in Table 5.5, more than three-fourth (87.44 per cent) of the educated unemployed respondents are worried about the prospect of employment. Just 12.57 per cent of the total 191 educated unemployed respondents, responding to the question "Are you worried about getting a job?" indicates that they are 'not' worried. Of the total 87.44 per cent who are worried for a job, about 8.90 per cent indicates that they are a 'little' worried, 39.27 per cent indicates 'somewhat' worried and 39.27 per cent indicates that they are 'very much' worried. It is obvious that an educated unemployed will not only be frustrated but very much worried when he is unemployed without any earning job for long period. He will not only be worried about the prospect of employment, but he will also blame self, the government and blame everybody. Firstly, an educated unemployed is worried, because he continues to be a parasite by depending everything on others. Secondly, he cannot support the

Table - 5.5

Educated Unemployed Youth concern for Occupational Future: by Faculties, Educational Qualification

Sl No	Faculty/Educational Qualification	Proportion of Educated Unemployed Youth who are:				Number	Total %
		i Not worried	Ii A little worried	iii Somewhat worried	iv Very much Worried		
1	Matriculate	0.00	(1) 6.66	**(7) 46.67**	**(7) 46.67**	15	100.00
2	Arts	(5) 11.36	(2) 4.55	(14) 31.82	**(23) 52.27**	44	100.00
3	Science	(4) 09.52	(5) 11.91	(14) 33.33	**(19) 45.24**	42	100.00
4	Commerce	(7) 17.07	(2) 4.88	**(20) 48.78**	(12) 29.27	41	100.00
5	Law	(4) 21.05	0.00	**(8) 42.11**	(7) 36.84	19	100.00
6	Engineering	(3) 18.75	0.00	(6) 37.50	**(7) 43.75**	16	100.00
7	Medicine	(1) 7.14	**(7) 50.00**	(6) 42.86	0.00	14	100.00
8	All Total	(24) 12.57	(17) 8.90	**(75) 39.27**	**(75)39.27**	191	100.00

family of which he is expected to do in completing education. Many of the educated unemployed are also worried and under much pressure to get any job immediately if they have to work in the government offices (state) as the age limit (30 years) is running out. Some of the educated job seekers are also worried for they have been denied of the jobs, which they thought they are qualified for, and in spite of all their efforts. Many educated job seekers have seen failures after failures. They are also worried for they know very well of the limited jobs available.

The educated unemployed of the 'not worried' category belongs to two sections - i) those that have just completed their studies or their period of unemployment are small, ii) and those from richer families. Many times the fresh unemployed fails to understand the stiffness of competition to get a job in the state. Again, it has been conceived that the richer the respondents' family the less likely he is to feel worried about his occupation. The family can permit him to be unemployed for a longer duration during which time he might be able to work out or grab jobs that are more satisfying. On the other hand, for the educated unemployed with limited means, the strategy is to find the job, satisfying or not, as soon as possible, and so he is worried.

Table 5.5 also clearly depicts the faculty-wise educated unemployed youth concern for their occupational future. The educated unemployed from the stream of arts, science and engineering has indicated 'very much worried' as the highest proportion, i.e. respectively arts (52.27 per cent), science (45.24 per cent) and engineering (43.75 per cent). Unemployed respondents from the stream of commerce and law have indicated 'somewhat worried' as the highest proportion, i.e. respectively commerce (48.75 per cent) and law (42.11 per cent). One-half (50.00 per cent) of the unemployed youth from the medicine faculty has indicated 'a little worried' as the highest proportion. In the matriculates' category, 46.67 per cent each has indicated 'somewhat worried' and 'very much worried' as the higher proportions. Therefore excluding medical, the educated unemployed respondents of all faculties showed considerable concern about unemployment - matriculates, engineering as well as arts, science as well as commerce and law.

This extent of concern for a job is also related to the perspective of job market where for instance, medical graduates are not worried or little worried as the job market for them is comparatively still high. It should be noted that all the respondents from the matriculates' category are worried about the prospect of employment.

It is also quite natural; that those who indicated they are worried has spent much more time thinking about their occupational plans. And not surprisingly, educated unemployed youth that are not worried about their job prospects spent much less time thinking about their occupational plans.

Table 5.6
Duration to Obtain Employment

Sl No.	Duration (in Years)	Number (%)
1•	0 – 1	16 (8.38)
2	1 – 2	20 (10.47)
3	2 – 3	18 (9.43)
4	3 – 4	12 (6.38)
5	4 – 5	08 (4.19)
6	More than 5 years	**25 (13.09)**

Note: Marked as uncertain/no idea/ can't say/don't know = 57 (29.84)
No comment = 35 (18.32).

The respondents' estimate of how long it will take them to obtain their first employment probably determines the extent of their worry. However almost half of the respondents are not certain how long it will take them for their first employment and so they have not commented or not marked the response. Exactly, 29.84 percent of the respondents has marked uncertain/no idea/can't say/ don't know against the question, and about 18.32 per cent remained silent with no comment. These respondents appear confused and frustrated with no hope to get any suitable job.

As shown in Table 5.6, the responses of the educated unemployed youth to the questionnaire indicated that about 8.38 per cent expected to get their first employment within a year, 10.47 per cent within 2 years, 9.43 per cent within 3 years, 6.28 per cent within 4 years, 4.19 per cent within 5 years and the highest 13.09 per cent indicates that it will take beyond 5 years to get a job. Therefore out of the marked responses, the maximum respondents have estimated that it will take more than 5 years or at least 5 years to get their first employment. And this is without restriction to any kind of job. Now if these educated unemployed who are already without a job for the last 3 years (mean period of unemployment = 2.63 years), and are going to take another 5 years to obtain employment, probably tells the extent of their worry. It clearly justifies why the majority of the unemployed respondents are not only worried but also very much worried. Perhaps those uncertain respondents must have purposively and intentionally omitted the question to save themselves from the embarrassment of their worry. The educated unemployed youth are therefore very much worried and under high pressure to get any available job. Again the certainty of getting a job has become a big question or who is going to get a job is also another issue. Related to this it is not surprising to hear a respondent saying "survival of the fittest" on being asked about his personal view regarding jobs.

In order to study the chief source of information about jobs, five categories of choices are listed in a separate question. It includes: i) news media, ii) employment experience of educated who has preceded you, iii) classroom discussion, friends, colleagues, iv) activities of guidance and employment bureau and v) any other. News media or newspaper advertisements (53.93 per cent) provide a major source of information about jobs. Accordingly, this is followed by activities of guidance and employment bureau (26.70 per cent); employment experience of educated who has preceded them (10.99 per cent); classroom discussion, friends and colleagues (5.76 per cent); and the least (2.62 per cent) has indicated 'any other' as the major source of information about the job market.

iv. Frequency of Job Attempts:

Out of the total 191 respondents, 122 respondents, that is, 63.87 per cent has tried for a job at least once at the time the research work was conducted. While the rest of the respondents i.e. 36.13 per cent has not tried for any job even once, or perhaps has tried but does not want to mention. It is also worth to note that almost all the youth keep trying for a job themselves, without relying much on the Employment Exchange notification - for 52.88 per cent indicates that it is not necessary to get registered in an Employment Exchange in order to get a job.

Table 5.7
Frequency of Job Attempts (Total Number = 122)

Sl No.	No. of times	Total in No. (%)
1	Once	12 (9.84)
2	Twice	**37 (30.33)**
3	Thrice	30 (24.59)
4	Four Times	12 (9.84)
5	Five Times	08 (6.55)
6	More than Five Times	23 (18.85)

Frequencies of the attempts made by the respondents to secure an employment show that 9.84 per cent of the educated unemployed youth have tried once before the study by the researcher, 30.33 per cent have tried twice, 24.59 per cent thrice, 9.84 per cent up to four times, 6.55 per cent up to five times, and 18.85 per cent have tried more than five times, but failed to secure any employment. The highest frequency of job attempts is twice with 30.33 per cent. The maximum of the respondents, that is, almost one-third of the sample have unsuccessfully attempted jobs for two times. However, the jobs attempted by these unemployed respondents are the same jobs or different jobs are not known. The data has also revealed that some unemployed youth have tried thrice, four times, five times and there are some of them who have even tried more than five times without success. To attempt job four times, five times, and even more than five times without any success surely speaks volume to the extent of their worry. Not only this, but one could question whether there is such an employment opportunity for a person who have seen failures five times or more in trying for jobs.

v. Perspective of Job Market:

More specifically, on the line of the above discussions, how do the educated youth view the job market? How do the unemployed youth estimate their probabilities of securing jobs? Which jobs do the unemployed feel, are likely to become available and which jobs will be hard to come by? These are some questions which needs to be discussed diligently. And responses of the educated youth to such questions perhaps might also represent a realistic appraisal of the situation in the state, or perhaps an unfounded hope that in their chosen field jobs will be available, or perhaps could indicate the extent to which the unemployed youth are able to correctly interpret the changing market trends. Since the classification of occupations adopted in the questionnaire is more specific, the analysis, therefore, represents the reactions of respondents to information they receive from different sources, rather than an accurate estimate of manpower needs.

The respondents are asked to estimate the incidence of unemployment among the educated youth (i.e. matriculate and above). Of which 83.77 per cent of the respondents estimated that more than 20 % of the educated youth must be unemployed. On a more personal level, respondents are asked about the present employment status of three best friends that has completed their studies in the recent past. That more than 50.00 per cent of the respondents indicated their friends remained unemployed for long stretches of time.

Therefore the picture is gloomy, and the educated unemployed youth, as discussed earlier, had blamed the government in the past for not getting a job, but are they helpless for they are also aware that the government would not be able to generate employment for all.

In spite of the gloomy picture, the respondents have a mixed opinion. About 27.22 per cent and 6.28 per cent respectively, believed that job opportunities would 'increase' and 'rapidly increase' in the next 5 years. These respondents perceive that the government will be able to create more job avenues in the near future. Therefore, their attitudes towards the government can be considered positive and hopeful. About 26.18 per cent of the respondents believed that the job opportunities in the next 5 years will 'remain the same'. However about 26.18 per cent and 14.14 per cent respectively believed that the job opportunities will 'somewhat decrease' and 'rapidly decrease' in the next 5 years. These unemployed respondents seem to have lost confidence in the government and their attitude is negative towards the government. However, in spite of the gloomy picture many educated unemployed youth remain hopeful.

Table 5.8

Educated Unemployed Youth's Views of the Job Opportunities.

Sl. No.	Occupations	Proportion of Educated Unemployed Youth's indicating that the Opportunities will - i Increase the most	ii Increase the least
1	Govt. Administrative, Executive Official	7.85	**43.47**
2	University Teacher	4.71	3.66
3	Secondary School Teacher	14.66	1.57
4	Higher Research Worker	8.90	3.14
5	Legal (Law) Practitioner	1.57	3.14
6	Engineer	0.52	19.37
7	Physician/Surgeon (Medicine)	5.24	1.57
8	Salesman/Business	**26.70**	1.57
9	Farming	3.14	12.57
10	Politician/Political Agents	2.62	5.24
11	Clerk	0.52	3.66
12	Editor/Journalist	2.62	0.52
13	Police/Military	19.90	0.52
14	Computers	1.05	0.00
	Total	100.00	100.00
	Number	191	191

The respondents are asked to rank a given list of occupations (14 occupations as shown in Table 5.8), where they expected the job opportunities will increase the most rapidly and least rapidly in the next 5 years. As depicted in the Table (Table 5.8), the respondents indicated that job opportunities will increase the 'most rapidly' in the Business/Salesman occupation (i.e. 26.70 per cent); while job opportunities will increase the 'least rapidly' in the occupation category - Government Administrative, Executive Official (i.e. 43.47 per cent) in the next 5 years. The educated unemployed youth perceive that in the next 5 years business opportunities will increase the most rapidly than any other occupation. Then one can question if job opportunities will be available in this area, why the unemployed youth still seek for government jobs only. Perhaps these educated youth do not have sufficient capital to start a business or perhaps business is the last option of their occupation.

Of the 14 occupations provided in the Table, there are 8 government occupations. And quite a considerable percentage of the educated unemployed respondents perceive the job opportunities will increase in 2 government occupations that is, police or military and secondary school teacher. It is also obvious that job opportunities as teachers will increase for the rapid growth of students necessarily might demand more teachers. However, this is directly related to the financial position of the state government or the private proprietors. As far as police and military are concerned, the respondents might have perceived by observing the recent recruitment in the state. The educated unemployed respondents on the other hand perceive the other 6 remaining occupations that job opportunities will not increase. For that matter, almost half of the respondents argue that job opportunities in the government sector especially in the categories of administrative, executive officials will increase the least.

Thus to conclude, the future of the educated unemployed is expected to be very bleak in view of the shrinking employment opportunities. The proportion of the main workers to total population in the state is decreasing in spite of the increasing population, increasing literacy rate, resulting to increasing unemployment among the educated. There is no balance between the number of students produced and the number of jobs available. The study has revealed that the unemployed youth has remained without any remunerative job for 3 years and they blame the government for not getting a job. The average frequency of job attempts by these educated youth is twice and the maximum respondents perceive that it will take another 5 more years to get a job. As discussed, the perspective of job market looks gloomy, though many educated youth remains hopeful. Under all this circumstances, the educated unemployed youth in the state are worried, very much worried about the prospect of employment.

6

Problems and Social Consequences of Unemployed Youth

In the previous chapter, we have discussed the extent of concern of the educated unemployed youth about the prospect of employment in the state. The present chapter studies about the specific problems faced by an educated youth due to unemployment. It studies the multi-social problems that beset the unemployed youth and its related social consequences in the society today. This chapter also tries to study the attitudes of the unemployed youth towards the job, towards the present educational system, towards the method of selection to various jobs, towards the government and attitude towards the employment exchanges.

In the present context, people are confused as to what to fear? And whom to fear? Some people fear a) unemployment, while there are others who fear b) the unemployed youth. The educated unemployed is a dangerous person. He can become dangerously vocal and influential to give constant threat to the security and stability of the state. He nurses a sense of personal injury and if the grievance is long continued and the numbers involved are large, the situation can become decidedly explosive. The unemployed persons belonging to this category are 'not dumb, driven cattle', but intelligent people, and will not accept an unenviable position lying down. It also involves the waste of the best of our human resources for these educated people to remain idle (Puttaswamaiah, 1977).

Today, the unemployed youth have become a problem in its own, for the society and the nation. Youth, the force and future of the nation have become perhaps the most vulnerable section of society. Perhaps it is the most neglected lot, which has lost all public sympathy. It is i) physically deprived, ii) morally depressed, iii) socially ridiculed iv) economically dependent and v) psychologically frustrated, which only has neglect and insult in its account (Bajpai, 1992). Most of the problems of the youth emanate from their unemployment and therefore, unfulfilled needs in the society. Today many problems beset the youth and these certainly need timely recognition.

Youth despite of all their energy and enthusiasm, merit and mission, aspirations and attempts, appears to be lost and deprived. In this regard, the study attempts to particularly deal with in this unit, a few questions like -

i) What is more, that an educated youth should possess to get a job?

ii) Who is responsible for this?

iii) Why is this so?

iv) What are the problems, the specific problems faced by educated unemployed? and

v) What are its social consequences?

vi) What are the reasons?

i. Problems:

Earlier studies have traced the problem of unemployment back to the Industrial Revolution, and more recently to the educational explosion. Nagas, though they were socially, economically, etc. backward before the advent of the British and its administration, yet the socio-economic system was free from the problems like unemployment. An imported system of education, which is meant for supporting clerical staff to the colonial rule, is blindly followed by the country and in all its states till today (Bajpai, 1992). The educated unemployment and many other problems faced by the state today are perceived to be the bye-product of its education system.

A Babu's job became a matter of craze for the Nagas especially after the statehood (on 1st Dec. 1963). The present young generation got mainly enchanted of the mirky lights of electronic gadgets. The present youth are no more interested in the paddy fields, in jhum fields, in any manual labour. Education has developed a kind of complex with the educated youth. Moreover, parents in the state expect their wards to get education. And therefore irrespective of the economic background the parents send their children to schools and colleges, which finally creates a large army of educated unemployed youth in the state. And unfortunately many of these educated unemployed youth have lost the dignity of labour, though in previous chapters we have discussed that they are ready for manual jobs in case of no other alternatives. Generally youth should have high ambitions, but in the state general goalessness is more visible among the youth. Very few educated youth plan and prepare for the future. There are many instances where many youths will be colliding with each other suddenly jumping in to the situation without any proper preparation and thinking. Many youths even fail to read their own capacity and ability, having ambitions that can never be fulfilled. Again, many educated youth in the state lack adventurism usually expected of them, rather they appear to be over-submissive, frustrated and an idle lot of Luddites.

The unemployment of the educated youth is not only a problem of theirs, but has become the problem of the family, the society, and the nation at large. After spending the hard-earned money of one's parents and about two decades of precious time, the educated youth finds himself at the crossroads. He is desperate for any kind of job but finds no one to buy him. And thus, every educated youth is humiliated in two ways:

i) *Firstly*, he can not contribute anything to the familial economy because he could not work during the course of his study.
ii) *Secondly*, his two decades devotion to education is a waste without any fruits.

Not only this, he finds himself answerable to the aspirations and expectations of the family. He is answerable to the family, who has spared everything on him, who has invested on him; its sweat earned income/money with a hope that he would emancipate the family from all socio-economic curses after his education.

Subjected to all this, and particularly subjected to the parent's expectations, he finds himself guilty. The study reveals that some of them do not even wish to go home and do not even want to meet their friends. He keeps avoiding everyone; he does not want to meet any one, as he does not have the courage. He feels like a 'death sentence' or a poison has been put under his throat when somebody asks him "what are you doing now-a-days?" A few of them has to work in unfavourable, inferior conditions and thus develops many psychological and health problems. The queues of educated people looking for jobs is growing longer day by day.

Colin (1972) lists seven features of bereavement of unemployed youth:

1. Realization of loss.
2. Alarm reaction.
3. Urge to search for and find lost object.
4. Anger and guilt.
5. Feeling an internal loss of self or mutilation.
6. Identification with symbols of a job.
7. Pathological variations of a grief.

Bajpai (1992) have lined down the following nine problems faced by an unemployed youth:

1. Loss of trust and support of the family.
2. Financial hardship.
3. Psychological problems like frustration, loss of self-esteem and self-confidence, depression, anxiety and the feeling of self-contempt.
4. Adjustmental problems - intra-personal and inter-personal, with family, society and peer groups.

5. Rejection by society.
6. Mal-nutrition and ill health.
7. Favouritism and corruption in the matters of employment.
8. Problem related to sex and marriage.
9. Problems related to identity formation.

These problems may be present individually, successively and collectively. Douglas and Driscoll (1973) have identified four stages that an unemployed person experiences: i) there is initially a period of relaxation and relief after completion of one's studies. ii) After a rest period, the person will enter the period of concerted efforts where he/she will energetically look for work. iii) When these efforts do not pay off and the person is still unemployed a period of vacillation and doubt, sets in and mood changes occur. iv) If this continues long enough and the person does not gain employment, he or she enters the period of malaise and cynicism.

Likewise, the educated unemployed youth of the state suffers from many (most) similar problems discussed above. In a nutshell, the unemployed youth of the state are faced with the following problems -

1. With high expectations from their wards, the parents send them to school, college, even in spite of many financial barriers. But the hopes of the parents seem belied. The parents, who expect a lean of support from their child, realize him as a burden over the family, even after completion of higher education. Therefore, the educated youth appears to be in 'loss of the trust' of the family, by being unemployed.
2. The unemployed youth develops a feeling of frustration, a feeling of self-contempt, guilt and looses self-confidence on the non-fulfillment of his family expectations. Though he highly regards his parental feelings and expectations, he finds himself incapable, despite his best efforts.
3. The unemployed youth fails to adjust with his friends, his family and the society. Many of them incur inter-personal conflicts due to which he either becomes idle or a rebel.

4. Due to his rebelling nature he faces dejection from the society, friends and even family members. He looses respect and sympathy of the people.
5. The educated unemployed feels deprived due to corruption, nepotism, and favouritism in the matters of employment. Their sentiments are grieved because of the biased method of selection. This has developed anger and guilt in the minds of the unemployed youth.
6. Due to overwhelming frustration and the feelings of worthlessness, it often leads to mal-nutrition and ill health of the youth.
7. The unemployed youth faces financial hardship. He wants to be independent but at the same time could not even meet his basic personal needs.
8. The unemployed youth suffers from identity formation and as a result identifies oneself with symbols of a job though they remain unemployed.

These are some of the striking problems faced by the educated unemployed youth pertaining to the state of Nagaland. Again some of these problems are further elaborated in detail below, in the form of the attitudes of unemployed youth towards various social aspects.

ii. Attitude of the Unemployed Youth:

In continuation with the discussion of the problems a few questions are asked to study the attitudes of the unemployed youth towards various facts of society. It is concerned with the attitudes of the unemployed youth in response to their unemployment towards various social aspects viz. the job, present educational system, method of selection, government, their family, their peer groups, political-infrastructure, self-employment, Employment Exchange, etc.

a) Attitudes towards the Job:

As already discussed in Chapter IV, on being asked the question, will you get a satisfactory job? About 22.51 per cent are confident of getting a satisfactory job, while 5.76 per cent firmly said no, about three-fourth i.e. 71.73 per cent of the respondents are not sure whether they will get a satisfactory job or not.

The most preferable job for these educated unemployed youth is government job. About 67.01 per cent of these unemployed respondents has marked government job as the most preferable job, about 6.81 per cent marked private jobs, while the remaining 26.18 per cent preferred self-employed jobs than any other jobs.

It is true that a specific type of education makes oneself eligible for a specific job, for example - professions like doctors, engineers, etc. However, to get a job, to get any kind of job seems to be everyone's ambition. The study reveals that more than three-fourths of these unemployed youths i.e. 83.25 per cent are ready for any kind of job, they are ready for even manual jobs. In other words they are not looking for a specific job. Only a minimal 16.75 per cent are not ready for manual jobs.

Table 6.1

Attitudes towards the Job.

Sl. No.	Statement	Responses in %		
		i Yes	ii No	iii Can't Say/ Don't Know
1	Every capable person should work because work is natural and dignified	**98.95**	0.00	1.05
2	I will go on trying for jobs without getting easily disappointed by failures.	**88.48**	5.76	5.76
3	I am confident that when the right time comes every one will get a suitable job.	34.56	**42.93**	22.51

In addition to the above discussion, Table 6.1 also gives ideas about the attitudes of the unemployed youth towards jobs. About 98.95 per cent have agreed that work is natural and dignified and therefore every capable person should work. The educated unemployed youth want job and want to work and they are capable.

But joblessness leads to idleness, rebellious nature and frustration, which further leads to all kinds of problems. Now despite the failures, about 88.48 per cent strongly agrees to keep on trying for jobs (any jobs) without getting easily disappointed, however only 34.56 per cent are confident of getting suitable jobs. About 42.93 per cent of the unemployed youth are not confident to get any suitable job even when the right time comes. These 42.93 per cent have lost confidence in themselves, over the employment system. This section of the educated unemployed population feels maximum deprivation, which will slowly develop into guilt and anger with oneself first and with everything afterwards that one faces.

b) Attitude about Present Educational System:

Studies conducted earlier elsewhere (Ahuja, Puttaswamaiah, Bajpai, etc.) have shown the youth's dissatisfaction with the present education system. These earlier studies are of the view that education itself creates unemployment because there is no application of University/College education in the society. The present education system even alienates the youth from their society. These studies show that the prevailing examination system is inappropriate and therefore, passing out these examinations makes no important contribution to secure a job. It suggests - since this examination cannot give any job and the actual test of students' knowledge is to be assessed by a competitive examination/test, there is no need for such a fake examination. But the present study reveals contradictory results.

It is observed from the Table (Table 6.2) that an average 56.98 percent-educated unemployed youth is satisfied with the present education system. In contradiction to earlier studies conducted in other states, the educated youth of this state opines that University courses still prepare the students for jobs (43.45 per cent). The Universities are not admitting too many students (59.69 per cent) and it is not a waste to give higher education to the youth even though there are no jobs available (78.01 per cent). The educated unemployed youth holds that though jobs are not offered to the students, the quality of education has not gone down. As depicted in the Table about 78.01 per cent of the respondents are satisfied

Table 6.2
Attitude about Present Educational System.

Sl No	Reasons / Statement	Responses in %		
		i Very Important	ii Somewhat Important	iii Unimportant/ Incorrect
1	It is a waste to give higher education to the youth when there are no jobs available.	18.33	3.66	**78.01**
2	Universities are admitting too many students compared to the number of jobs available.	21.99	18.32	**59.69**
3	University courses do not prepare students for jobs.	23.04	33.51	**43.45**
4	Jobs are not offered to the students because of the quality of education has gone down.	4.71	17.28	**78.01**
5	Political interference with the Universities has contributed to the decline of standards.	**45.55**	41.88	12.57
6	Education through a foreign medium prevents development of talent.	7.85	21.99	**70.16**
	Average Response	121.47/6 = 20.25	136.64/6 = 22.77	341.89/6 = **56.98**

with the quality of education. However, about 45.55 per cent of the unemployed youth are of the view that the education standard has declined due to the political interference with the universities.

As far as the medium of instruction is concerned, only a meager 7.85 per cent are not satisfied with the foreign medium (i.e. English), while 70.16 per cent educated youth are satisfied with the English medium of instruction.

c) Attitude towards the Method of Selection:

The method of selection to various jobs is not appropriate as it is biased towards the rich and the bureaucrats. The government is claiming to make policies for everyone, but about 84.82 per cent respondents are of the view that these policies benefit the rich sections only.

Table 6.3
Method of Selection/Corruption

Sl No	Statement	Responses in %		
		i Yes	ii No	iii Cant' Say Don't Know
1	Government claims to make policies for everyone but they benefit the rich sections only.	**84.82**	4.71	10.47
2	Persons who are rich should not bother about employment.	23.56	**63.35**	13.09
3	In the present condition one must use fair or unfair means to get a job.	**57.59**	30.89	11.52
4	The condition of the society today is such that those who have money and influence can easily get a job in society.	**95.82**	2.61	1.57
5	Even a poor student without money and influence can easily get a job in society.	13.61	**73.70**	13.09

After completing their studies/degrees, about 63.35 per cent respondents agreed that employment is a necessity whether one is rich or poor. In chapter IV, we find that the educated unemployed youth regard achievement criteria (i.e. education, hard work, ability) to be the most important factor for getting a satisfactory job. Factors like bribery and luck are not perceived as important and primary options. But on being denied of employment for long, under the present conditions, about 57.59 per cent respondents are willing to use any means (fair or unfair) to secure a job. Corruption and favouritism in the process of selection is unanimously, accepted by the respondents. Unanimously the respondents are of the view that 'money' and 'influence' has unfortunately become the formula to procure a job (95.82 per cent). A poor student without money and influence has very limited chance of getting a job in the present system (73.30 per cent). This practice/formula of procuring a job has become the norm of the day.

d) Attitude towards the Government:

The educated unemployed respondents are not satisfied with the government. It means they are not satisfied with the administrators and policy makers, policy planners, political leaders who are in power and have the power. They are not only dissatisfied but they even blame the government responsible of their unemployment as discussed earlier.

The educated unemployed youth expects some positive and concrete steps from the government to curb the problem of unemployment. Like an industry could be a governmental machinery where lots of educated youth could find solution to their hunger for jobs. But Nagaland is a poor state with no industry and the educated unemployed youth (75.92 per cent) unanimously agreed to it. Again, unfortunately the state government could not maintain few small industries, which we have, like Tuli Paper Mill, Dimapur Sugar Mill that has to be closed down. The respondents (76.44 per cent) are convinced that the government is not doing enough in promoting/setting up industries in the state. This is also a clear indication that the administrators and policy makers have not paid enough attention to the problem of unemployment (67.02 per cent). Still more political leaders have not shown enough courage in dealing with unemployment (65.97 per cent). But against the statement - the government collaborates to keep unemployment high - is incorrect according to 68.06 per cent of the respondents.

Table 6.4
Attitude towards the Government

Sl No.	Statement / Reason	Responses (%)		
		Very Important	Somewhat Important	Unimportant/ Incorrect
1	No industry to absorb the educated unemployed youth.	**75.92**	14.66	9.42
2	The government has not gone far enough in promoting/setting up industries.	**76.44**	14.66	8.90
3	Administrators and policy makers have not paid enough attention to the problem of unemployment.	**67.02**	29.32	3.66
4	Political leaders have not shown courage in dealing with unemployment.	**65.97**	30.89	3.14
5	The government collaborates to keep unemployment high.	12.57	19.37	**68.06**
6	Improper utilization of funds leads to stagnation of development.	**90.58**	8.90	0.52
7	The various governmental departments do not properly notify vacant jobs.	**78.01**	17.80	4.19

The various funds and schemes that are meant for development and advancement of the state have been misused. For that matter about 90.58 per cent of the respondents blame the government for stagnation of development due to improper utilization of funds. This directly affects the educated unemployed youth for stagnation of any society forbids employment opportunities. Again, 78.01 per cent of the respondents agreed that the various governmental departments do not properly notify vacant jobs.

e) Attitude towards Employment Exchange:

After World War II, in 1945 the Directorate General of Employment and Rehabilitation has been established in order to provide employment and rehabilitation to released soldiers, under which Employment Exchanges are established all over the country. In 1959, Indian Parliament passed Employment Exchange (compulsory notification of vacancies) Act that came into effect from May 1960. The name of the Directorate General of Rehabilitation and Employment is changed to Directorate General of Employment and Training (Bajpai, 1992).

At present there are 1 Regional Employment Exchange, 6 District Employment Exchange, 2 Rural Employment Bureau, 1 Coaching-cum-Guidance Centre, 2 Industrial Training Institute, 1 Women Industrial Training Institute, 1 Self Employment Promotion Cell, and 1 Physically Handicapped Cell in the state of Nagaland.

Unfortunately Employment Exchanges are not serving in the manner, as conceived in the beginning. They have rather reduced to be white elephants (Bajpai, 1992). They do not cover all the unemployed persons, being registering in Employment Exchange voluntary. The registration is mainly concentrated in urban areas and many have not registered in the Employment Exchange, as it is not effective according to them. Though vacancies are notified through the Employment Exchange, the employers are not bound to select out of those sent through it. Apart from notifying vacancies in Employment Exchange, they are free to advertise in other Newspapers and Employment News Bulletins. Thus, the very purpose of Employment Exchange has got defeated. Thus there is no benefit from registration in Employment Exchange. Again, ironically enough, not all the vacancies are notified, rather a few categories of jobs are only notified to Employment Exchange.

In western countries, graduate students register themselves with Employment Department because they get 'unemployed allowance' on maturity, but no such 'benefits' are provided to Indian youth, consequently, only a slight fragment of unemployed get registered with Employment Exchanges. As a matter of fact, about 60.73 per cent of the respondents are of the view that at least the government should provide unemployment allowance.

Table 6.5

Distribution of sample by registration and Period of registration with the Employment Exchange

i	ii	iii
Registered	Not Registered	Total
105 (54.97)	86 (45.03)	191

Period of registration (total = 105).

Period (in years) Registered	Number	% Against Total
0 – 1	16	15.24
1 – 2	18	17.14
2 – 3	12	11.43
3 – 4	14	13.33
4 – 5	20	19.05
More than 5 yrs (up to 15 years)	**25**	**23.81**

Mode Period = more than 5 years.

As given in Table 6.5, 54.97 per cent of the respondents have registered in Employment Exchange, while 45.03 per cent of the respondents have not registered. In a separate question, the respondents view is recorded whether it is necessary to get registered in an Employment Exchange in order to get a job. Of which, 52.88

per cent are of the view that it is not necessary to get registered to secure employment. It therefore indicates that out of 54.97 per cent registered respondents, 7.85 per cent respondents have registered though they know it is not necessary. They might have registered under the pressure of family members, relatives or under the influence of friends, but have not registered willingly. Thus, in actual term more than one-half of the sample respondents perceive Employment Exchange as not necessary in order to get a job, which clearly depicts its ineffectiveness as already discussed in Chapter II.

The period of registration of these registered respondents is also clearly shown in the same Table. And the highest frequency with 23.81 per cent for the period of registration is in the category 'more than five year. The validity of every registration is 3 years and has to be renewed after every 3 years. Of these registered respondents, the data reveals that 59 respondents (56.19 per cent) have at least renewed once. It is therefore quite sure that more than one-half of these respondents have remained unemployed for a long time and the Employment Exchange failed to help them. Again, those respondents whose period of registration is up to 15 years must have at least renewed their registration 5 times. This long period of registration once again speaks volume of negligence and ineffectiveness of the Employment Exchanges in the state.

iii. Family and Related Problems:

Sociologically speaking family is the heart of social life. It is evident from the Table (Table 6.6) that the education and career of the children / of the educated youth is always taken care of by the father or the family (94.76 per cent). The parents of these respondents spend money not only for acquiring knowledge (59.15 per cent) but to get a good job too (35.61 per cent). At the same time as already discussed the parents have high expectations from these educated respondents, while 26.18 per cent of the respondents feel frustrated for they cannot satisfy or fulfill these expectations.

It is also evident from the same Table that about 55.50 per cent are from poor families. And as such their parents could not spend much on their education and job trials. However, 56.54 per cent of the respondents are of the view that their parents give or will give freely money for jobs and attending interviews irrespective of

Table 6.6
Educated Unemployed Youth and Family Related Problems

Sl No.	Statement	i Yes	ii No	iii Don't Know/ Can't Say
1	My father/family has never taken interest in my education and career matters.	4.19	**94.76**	1.05
2	My parents spend money for my education to get a good job more than to acquire knowledge.	35.61	**59.15**	5.24
3	Expectations of my parents/relatives are too high for me to satisfy/fulfill.	26.18	**60.73**	13.09
4	As I am from a poor family, my parents cannot spend much on my education and job trials.	**55.50**	36.65	7.85
5	My parents gives or will freely give money for jobs or attending interviews.	**56.54**	29.32	14.14
6	My family complains of my unemployment.	31.94	**60.83**	7.33
7	My family members sympathize with me for being unemployed.	**56.02**	2.18	17.80
8	I cannot hope to get a job without my family's help and support.	**58.12**	31.93	9.95
9	Unemployment among educated youth socially taxes the aspirations of parents and relatives.	**73.30**	5.23	21.47

family background. Though 60.83 per cent of the respondents' parents do not complain about their unemployment, it is not surprising to note that 31.94 percent complains about the unemployment of the respondents. And this second section of the educated unemployed youth appears to be in 'lost of the trust' of the family by being unemployed. In spite of remaining unemployed, 56.02 per cent of the family members still sympathize with the educated unemployed.

About 73.30 per cent of the respondents are of the view that unemployment among the educated youth socially taxes the aspirations of parents and relatives. But whatever be the matter, about 58.12 per cent of the respondents cannot hope to get a job without the help and support of the family.

iv. Social Consequences:

The social consequences are related to the various problems faced by the unemployed youth. In other words, it is often the outcome of the problem that has been long harboured and suffered. It is essential to discuss the social problems along with its related social consequences. Many of the related consequences have been featured already in the discussion of the problems above. This section of the study discusses some of the more severe consequences of the problem of youth unemployment.

Youth are the human property of the nation; they represent strength, vitality and vigour and are the hope for the future of a nation. But if these youth remains idle, worried and inactive due to unemployment and is forced to do something to become an earning hand, he usually does not care for the social norms and values and becomes subject to many kinds of vices as indulgence into drug addiction etc. True is the Sanskrit idiom; "Bubhukshitah Kim Na Karoti Papam" meaning thereby a hungry man can do any sin (Bajpai, 1992).

In view of 90.05 per cent of the unemployed youth, unemployment frustrates youth's ambitions. The educated unemployed youth are temperamentally frustrated, impatient, and restless (79.06 per cent). It is found that the respondents feel bored on account of unemployment; dull and the feelings of self-contempt and self-distrust develops. It is difficult even for a strong man to keep his self-respect (77.49 per cent) and the unemployed youth will have the feeling that he is not well treated by his people (51.31 per cent).

Table 6.7
Unemployment and Social Consequences.

Sl No.	Social Consequences	% Response (Yes)
1	Unemployment frustrates youth's ambitions.	90.05
2	Educated unemployed youth are temperamentally frustrated, impatient, restless, etc.	79.06
3	Unemployment leads to family disorganization, disunity and discord among the family.	65.44
4	The problem of unemployment disrupts peace with neighbours.	62.31
5	Educated unemployment is a serious threat to the society.	97.38
6	Educated unemployment has contributed to the spread of drugs, alcoholism, smuggling and drug trafficking.	70.70
7	Educated unemployment takes to anti-social activities like bandits, highway robberies, extortionists, etc.	67.54

It is accepted by 65.44 per cent that unemployment leads to family disorganization, disunity and discord among the family. About 62.31 per cent of the respondents are of the view that the problem of unemployment disrupts peace with neighbours. Educated unemployment is a serious threat not only to the family, or neighbours, but is a serious threat to the society (97.38 per cent) today.

As given in the Table, it is accepted by 70.70 per cent of the respondents that educated unemployment has contributed to the spread of drugs and alcoholism, smuggling and drug trafficking too.

The respondents (67.54 per cent) believe that due to unemployment, the educated unemployed youth are taking to anti-social activities. These anti-social activities include bandits, highway robbers, extortionists, etc. It can be therefore concluded that the youth has become economically vulnerable; thereby they are increasingly getting into the trap of violence.

The youth of today expects white-collar job and does not like to take risks. He is becoming less adventurous and wants a steady income. He wants to be prosperous and luxurious through a salaried job. There is a general disinclination among the educated youth to look for employment other than the government job (69.63 per cent). About 35.08 per cent of the educated unemployed look only for government jobs. Self-employment jobs are given a low priority, as against paid government jobs (73.30 per cent).

It is accepted only by 6.28 per cent of the respondents that unemployed are not good enough to find jobs, and they seek jobs generally beyond their ability (11.32 per cent). It is also accepted by 9.42 per cent of the respondents that many educated do not want to work and thus, they remain unemployed while they wait for better jobs (19.90 per cent).

Again, some are not employed because they would not like to work regarding certain jobs or in certain places (75.92 per cent).

To conclude, the problem of unemployment among the educated youth is one of the gravest that the state faces today. Personally, they appear to be in 'lost of the trust' of the family, and have lost even respect and sympathy of the people. The educated youth develops a feeling of frustration, self-contempt, guilt and looses self-confidence due to long years of unemployment. The unemployed youth fails to adjust with his friends, his family and the society. They face financial hardships. And all this has resulted in severe consequences. It has invited the anger of our youth and they are increasingly indulging into illegal, anti-social and other violent and criminal activities too. And this is the expression of their distrust to the system. The deprivations in the matters of recruitment further generate socio-economic problems like corruption, nepotism, favouritism, etc.

Therefore, the problem of unemployment among the educated youth is a serious problem that needs timely attention and solution. Determined efforts are needed and appropriate policies are to be made so that our young men and women can become job creators and not remain job seekers.

7

Opinions on Self-Employment

In the previous chapter, we have discussed the multi-social problems faced by the educated unemployed youth and its related social consequences in the society. The attention of the study in this unit is towards the policies and programmes directly concerned with employment-promotion, the various schemes of self-employment for the youth, especially the educated youth. The study attempts to deal with a few questions like - i) Are the self-employment schemes sufficient enough for educated unemployed youth? ii) Are the funds/ loans/money sufficient enough for the projects? iii) Are the right persons/right educated unemployed youth benefited from the various self-help schemes/projects? iv) Are the various schemes/ loans of self-employment projects properly utilized? v) Are the educated unemployed beneficiaries really taking up the projects? vi) Is the government really serious in solving educated unemployment problem? However, the study presented is solely the view points/opinions of the respondents and thus the data/information constraints do not permit firm generalizations.

i. Employment Promotion Programmes:

Employment-promotion programmes has been divided into two sets: i) one dealing with employment-promotion for people in general which includes the youth of the country and ii) the second set directly, and exclusively, approaching the problem of youth unemployment (Chadha, 2000). Likewise there are a number of employment-promoting programmes directed specifically at the educated youth and directed at people in general in the state. A few of them operating in the state of Nagaland are:

i. **SEEUY:**

The Self-Employment Scheme for Educated Unemployed Youth launched in 1983-84. It aims at providing financial assistance to unemployed youth, to the educated unemployed youth for undertaking economically viable activities.

ii. **PMRY:**

This programme (Prime Minister Rozgar Yojna), launched on October2, 1993, has been designed to provide self employment to more than a million of educated unemployed youth in the age-group of 18 to 35 years, (by setting up seven lakh micro enterprises during the Eight Plan), through the industry, service and business routes. The scheme also sought to associate reputed NGO's in the implementation of PMRY, especially in the selection and training of would-be entrepreneurs and in the preparation of project profiles.

It began as an urban programme in 1993 but just after a year, it encompassed both rural and urban areas.

Projects up to Rs. 1 lakh are covered under the scheme in the case of individuals. If two or more eligible persons joined together in a partnership, projects of higher cost would also be covered. For availing financial assistance for the project, the prospective entrepreneur is required to contribute only 5 per cent of the project cost; the rest came through institutional loans. The central government provides a subsidy @ 15 per cent of the project cost subject to a ceiling of Rs 7500 per entrepreneur.

The schemes stipulate compulsory stipendiary training for a period of 15 to 20 working days for service/business sectors, after the loan is sanctioned. The department of small-scale industries has framed suitable training modules for industry and service/business sectors.

iii. **IRDP:**

Integrated Rural Development Programme and its allied activities are major self-employment programmes for poverty alleviation. The basic objective of IRDP is to enable the identified rural families to create avenues of self-employment through the acquisition of credit-based productive assets and inputs, which generate additional employment on a sustained basis. Assistance is given in the form of subsidy by the government and term credit by the financial institutions for income generating activities. The scheme has been in operation in Nagaland since 1983-84.

This is a centrally sponsored scheme funded on 50:50 bases by the centre and the states. It is stipulated that at least 50 per cent of the assisted families should be women.

iv. TRYSEM*:*

Training of Rural Youth for Self-Employment (TRYSEM) is a facilitating component of poverty-eradication programme - IRDP. It aims at providing basic technical and entrepreneurial skills to the rural poor in the age group of 18 to 35 years to enable them to take up self- or image-unemployment. At least 40 per cent of the beneficiaries have to be women.

Training is imparted through both training institutions and through the non-institutionalized mode, e.g. master craftsmen functioning from their own place of work. Every TRYSEM trainee becomes eligible to avail of assistance under IRDP for setting up a self-employment enterprise.

v. SGSY*:*

Swarnjayanti Gram Swarozgar Yojana (SGSY) is another centrally sponsored scheme introduced in the state during the year 1999-2000 with the objective of bringing every assisted poor family above the poverty line within three years through the provision of micro-enterprise. The poverty alleviation programmes are clubbed together into these schemes which includes all IRD programmes i.e. a) IRDP and its component TRYSEM which we have already discussed above, b) DWCRA, c) GKY, d) MWS and Tool Kits.

During the year 1999-2000, a sum of Rs 120.00 lakh as state share and a sum of Rs 380.00 lakh as central share is spent as anticipated. Out of this, 165 SHG are formed and assisted for taking up various micro-enterprises and 1250 individual Swarozgaris are assisted.

vi. **JRY:**

This programme (Jowahar Rozgar Yojana) has been launched on April 1, 1989, as a centrally sponsored scheme. Its main objective is the generation of additional gainful employment for unemployed and underemployed people, both men and women, in the rural areas through the creation of rural economic infrastructure, community and social assets, with the aim of improving the quality of life of the rural poor, which include the beneficiaries themselves. At least 30 per cent of the employment is to be provided to woman. In practice, the programme is self-targeting.JRY since April 1, 1999, has been renamed Jawahar Gram Samridhi Yojana (JGSY). The new JGSY programme is dedicated entirely to the development of rural infrastructure at the village level and is implemented by the village panchayats.

During the year 1999-2000, an amount of Rs 210.00 lakh as state share and Rs 630.00 lakh as central share giving a total of Rs 840.00 lakh was spent as anticipated. This fund is utilized for household allocation to the VDBs @ Rs. 500 per household allocation. It has also earmarked 7.5 per cent for training of VDB functionaries and honorarium for VDBs secretaries.

vii. **EAS:**

The Employment Assurance Scheme (EAS) is another centrally sponsored scheme operating in the state. During 1999-2000 an amount of Rs 558.00 lakh as state share being 25 per cent of the total allocation of the programme and an amount of Rs 1674 lakh as central share is spent as anticipated.

viii. **IAY:**

The Indira Awas Yojana is another programme that is operating in the state with the objective of helping the targeted poor people in constructing houses. During the year 1999-2000, an amount of Rs 145.00 lakh has been earmarked as state share and Rs. 435.00 lakh as central matching share has been proposed making a total of Rs 580.00 lakh. And it is targeted to construct about 4'000 houses in the state.

In addition to normal IAY, a sum of Rs 40.00 lakh is kept for use for the new credit-cum-subsidy scheme (IAY) where the state and the centre contribute on the basis of 75:25 ratio which is given to the beneficiaries at the rate of Rs 10'000 per household to those identified beneficiaries who can raise an amount of Rs 40'000 as loan from any financial institutions.

ix. Grants - Aid to VDBs:

During the year 1999-2000 a total amount of Rs 1125.00 lakh has been earmarked to be allocated to the VDBs @ Rs 750 per household to take up socio-economic programmes as well as basic infrastructures.

x. BMS:

Basic Minimum Services (BMS) is a new programme introduced by the government of India in 1996-1997. The main objective of the programme is to bridge the gap in infrastructural sector as well as for economic development of the people. The Rural Development Department is implementing the BMS under two sectors: a) Rural Housing and b) Road Connectivity.

a) *Rural Housing*: During the year 1999-2000, an amount of Rs 669.00 lakh has been earmarked and out of which a total of 4700 number of houses is expected to be constructed.

b) *Road Connectivity*: A total of 125 villages have been identified having no linking road as yet, for which the department constructs the roads. In spite of the state's financial constraints, the state government has been kind enough to provide extra amounts whenever necessary.

Therefore, these schemes as discussed above are some of the programmes operating in the state of Nagaland. And most of these schemes as discussed are jointly sponsored by the central government and the state government where implementation of the projects is the responsibility of the state government. It also has to be noted that many of these programmes are not directly employment promotion programmes but has to do more with the development of the rural masses. However the success of the various schemes operating in the state, proper implementation of the projects, identification of beneficiaries and areas, etc. has become a public debate especially among the circles of educated youth.

ii. Opinions on Self-Employment Schemes:

Table 7.1 below has been presented to study the preferences of the educated unemployed respondents about the nature of job. This Table is arranged in order to assess the opinions of the educated unemployed youth towards the self-employed jobs and the self-employment schemes. The findings confirm that about 67.01 per cent of the educated youth most preferable job is government service, about 26.18 per cent youth preferred self-employed jobs, and about 6.81 per cent educated youth preferred private jobs. The findings of the study conducted in Uttar Pradesh by Bajpai (1992) puts the self-employed jobs (8 per cent) at the last cadre of preference. However, the present study reveals that the self-employed jobs (26.18 per cent) are better preferred at least above the private jobs (6.81 per cent). In other words, the educated youth of the state of Nagaland has better favourable attitude towards self-employment as compared to the state of Uttar Pradesh.

Table 7.1
Preferences towards Self-Employment.

Sl. No.	Most Preferable Job	Total in Number	Total in %
1	Government Jobs	128	67.01
2	Self-Employed Jobs	50	26.18
3	Private Jobs	13	6.81
	Total	191	100.00

The educated unemployed youth preferences for government jobs as discussed in earlier chapters are that the youth wants security of service and stability of employment. It may be summarized that social recognition of government service is another factor to motivate the youth for it. Again, it appears that most of these educated youth do not want to take any entrepreneur risk involved in the self-employment, and therefore, they give very less priority. Many educated unemployed youth lack entrepreneurship zeal, lack entrepreneurial skill and at the same time they do not allow outsiders to invest freely.

Further, the findings confirmed that about 96.34 per cent of the educated youth would take up self-employment programmes if they were given help. But only a meager 8.90 per cent had so far tried for self-employment schemes. And this has presented a dubious question which perhaps needs an in depth study etc. It could also be that the majority of the unemployed youth do not know about many self-employment schemes, or are not aware of many schemes, which are meant for them. Many respondents are of the opinion that the help rendered by the government is insufficient to start any self-employment project. Again, many who know about the schemes have argued that the schemes are not running fairly and a number of mal-practices are involved in issuing the grant such as commission pay-offs, wrong selection of beneficiaries, undue delay, etc. Of the 17 respondents (i.e. 8.90 per cent), who have tried for self-employment schemes/projects, 06 have tried for SEEUY, 04 have tried JRY, 02 tried Departmental schemes and the other 05 have tried other schemes not listed in the questionnaire. These 8.90 per cent of the respondents have tried for loan under various self-unemployment schemes, but they could not secure it due to lack of conformity with the mal-practices involved.

Further, going by the responses of the educated unemployed youth in the questionnaire, the self-employment schemes that are operating in the state of Nagaland seems to be by and large, a complete failure. *Firstly*, about 49.22 per cent of the educated respondents' responds that the self-employment projects are 'not sufficient' for the educated unemployed youth, while 22.51 per cent responded that it is 'not at all sufficient'. Only 26.70 per cent of the educated unemployed youth responded that the projects are 'just sufficient', while a meager 1.57 per cent agrees that the projects for educated unemployed youth are 'fully sufficient'. And the finding is obvious, because only a few hundreds are benefited from the self-employment schemes out of the so many thousands of educated unemployed youth in the state. The self-employment schemes are not at all sufficient.

Table 7.2
Opinions on Self-Employment Schemes

Sl. No.	Statement	Yes	No	Not Sure
1	The funds (money) are enough/ sufficient for the projects.	27.33	72.77	-
2	The right persons/right educated unemployed are benefited from the various self-help schemes/ projects.	30.37	69.63	-
3	The various schemes/loans of self-employment projects are properly utilized.	0.00	64.92	35.08
4	The educated unemployed beneficiaries are really taking up the projects.	19.90	80.10	-

Secondly, as depicted in Table 7.2, about 72.77 per cent of the educated respondents are of the view that the funds (money) provided for the programmes are not sufficient enough to carry out the projects. Generally the self-employment schemes includes some subsidies and loans which have to be returned in due time. And many times, most of the beneficiaries land in trouble as their project fails and at the same time they have to repay the loans. Questions relating to the technology of production and marketing - the projects are not technologically hooked-up with modern industrial enterprises - and thus it invites its own failure in the open and competitive market. *Thirdly*, about 69.63 per cent of the educated unemployed respondents agreed that the right persons/right educated unemployed youth are not benefited from the various self-help schemes. Therefore, the weakness of the programme, most notoriously, the identification of beneficiaries and the provision of credit has been a matter of great public debate. Many beneficiaries under various schemes are actually ineligible on various counts including age and educational qualifications, apart from already having business or being employed. The respondents unanimously agreed that the main beneficiaries of the scheme are local politicians and other Luddites. The study has also found out that some beneficiaries got schemes/loans twice at the cost of all other beneficiaries.

Fourthly, the loans (money) provided for self-employment are not properly utilized (64.92 per cent). The schemes seem futile as most of the unemployed persons are interested to digest the money subsidy and not in the success of the project. And *fifthly*, about 80.10 per cent of the respondents are of the view that the educated unemployed beneficiaries are not really taking up the projects. Some schemes begin and end with the provision of short-term training in different trades. Again, some schemes are often unrelated to the trend and growth of the local economy. In a majority of cases, no follow-up is built into the scheme.

The Indian experience shows that each intervention has to meet the specific requirements of the specified target groups. a) For some categories of people, self-employment is the right answer, while b) for some others; wage-employment needs to be propped up. For promoting self-employment, i) training and skill-up gradation seem to suffice in some cases. ii) But, in some, capital assistance is a must, while in iii) few other situations, market support remain the most crucial element (Chadha, 2000). Moreover, self-employment schemes are just one alternative, not the entire solution of unemployment or educated unemployment.

To conclude in brief, the employment schemes have failed due to:

a) Inadequate resource allocation needed for achieving the objectives.

b) Wrong identification of beneficiaries.

c) Lack of dedication to the job assigned.

d) Improper utilization of funds.

e) Lack of commitment on the part of the people to execute the programmes.

f) Lack of political and administrative will and

g) Lack of sympathy for the poor.

In all these schemes, the government has been the key agency for formulating the policies and implementing the programmes based on these policies. But since experiences vary from scheme to scheme, due importance should also be given to those agencies outside the government like the NGO's etc. which could be more successful and more durable. Therefore, a careful system of selection, proper training, and identification of trade/skills related to local economy, financial support, and marketing arrangements should not be handicapped by the politics and the bureaucratic system of implementation.

8

Conclusion

The problem of the educated unemployed constitutes a very serious and menacing problem. It has become the first rate state problem. When young men find they have to wait for years to get employment, they feel greatly upset. The educated youth seek a stable life but cannot secure it; they are hungry for opportunities, recognition and status. They feel that instead of sympathy and consideration, they have to bear derogatory remarks. Their vast energies and labour force, intelligence and knowledge are being wasted and untapped. Youth, the force and future of the nation has become perhaps the most vulnerable section of society. Perhaps it is the most neglected lot, which has lost all public sympathy. It is i) physically deprived, ii) morally depressed, iii) socially ridiculed, iv) economically dependent and v) psychologically frustrated which only has neglect and insult in its account. Many problems beset the youth of today and these certainly need timely recognition.

Today, the unemployed youth have become not only a problem in its own, but also a problem for the society and the nation at large. And in this context, people are confused as to what to fear and whom to fear? Whether to fear unemployment or the unemployed? The educated youth is an intelligent person and can become dangerously vocal and influential not to accept any unenviable position lying down and can give constant threat to the security and stability of the state. He nurses a sense of personal injury and if the grievance is long continued and the members involved are large, the situation is decidedly explosive.

The educated youth despite of all their energy and enthusiasm, merit and mission, aspirations and attempts is lost and deprived. In this regard the study attempts a few questions like- i) What is it that an educated youth should possess to get a job? ii) Who is responsible for this? iii) Why is this so? iv) What are the multi-social problems, the specific problems faced by an educated unemployed? v) What are the related social consequences? vi) Is the government really serious in solving the problem? vii) Does the government have any policy at all to curb this problem? viii) Is there any nearness to balance between the number of students produced and the number of jobs available?

The National Policy on Youth in 1998 came up with an objective 'Bekari Hatao' (Banish Unemployment). It also declared some other objectives which include like 'to instill in the youth a deep awareness of and respect for the principles and values, qualities of discipline, a scientific temper in the modes of thinking and action' etc. The present study reveals that these values and objectives have been ruined. 'Bekari Hatao' is only a utopian cry and has become a tool of the politicians to woo the young voters to obtain their dubious objectives. The golden period of life that one should enjoy in constructive pursuit is spent in sheer frustration, social-dejection and deprivation. When the youth have lost their relevance there can be no justice and fair play in their social life. Then no amount of policies and excellent combination of words can instill in the youth a commitment to the principles and values of life.

Salient Findings of the Study:

The study has found out that most of the educated unemployed youth in the sample come from middle class families with stable income above Rs 5'000 per month. Most of the respondents' fathers are mainly clerical workers and administrators who have matriculated, while most of the mothers are housewives and illiterates. The sample has 54.97 percent registered educated unemployed youth in the Employment Exchanges, while 45.03 per cent have not registered.

The sample contains 36.65 per cent female, and 63.35 per cent male unemployed youth, where 23.04 per cent respondents are from the arts faculty, 21.99 per cent represents science faculty, 21.47 per cent from the commerce faculty, 9.95 per cent from law, 8.38 per cent from the engineering and 7.33 per cent sample from the medicine stream. The mean age of the respondents is found to be 24.51 per cent years consisting pre-dominantly of unmarried educated youth with 92.67 per cent. There are 96 per cent Christians with 71.73 per cent belonging to nuclear families while the mean of the family size is 7.58 members. It is noted that the mode period of registration in Employment Exchange is more than 5 years.

There is an alarming rise of unemployment among the educated youth in Nagaland. The total number of job seekers on the Live Register that is 22'069 in 1991 has risen to 37'090 in 2000 (i.e. in a decade) at an increased percentage of 68.06 per cent taking 1991 as the base. The number of educated unemployed (matriculation plus) has increased from 10'534 in 1991 to 22'119 in 2000 at the increased rate of 109.98 per cent. The study reveals that in 10 years the percentage share of educated against the total unemployed constitutes always above 50 per cent (except in 1991 - 47.73 per cent) and stands at 59.64 per cent in 2000. And obviously, the highest numbers of educated unemployed are below graduate category standing at 85.67 per cent in 2000.

In spite of the increasing trend of unemployment, the number of vacancies notified and placement made has declined. Therefore, the probability of an unemployed person to get a job in the state is very low. In 2000, as against 37'090 registered job seekers, only 339 vacancies are notified and 73 placements are made through the Exchange, thus indicating 508 persons for a single job. It clearly indicates the seriousness of the problem where 98 persons for one job in 1991 have increased to 508 persons for one job in 2000.

In Kohima District, the number of job seekers on the Live Register, which is 12,064 in 1991, has increased at the rate of 43.37 per cent to 17,296 in 2000. While the number of educated unemployed has increased at the rate of 100.39 per cent from 6,333 in 1991 to 12,690 in 2000. The study finds out that the percentage share of educated against the total unemployed in the district has steeply increased to above 70.00 per cent from 1997 onwards. The educated unemployed in the district constitutes 60.78 per cent matriculates, 23.46 per cent pre-university, 14.59 per cent graduates, and only 1.17 per cent post-graduates in 2000. The study depicts that from 1991-2000, educated unemployed males constitutes the larger proportion than females in the district. Once again, the probability of an unemployed person to get a job is very low.

The study has revealed that more than half of the educated as well as the total registered job seekers on the Live Register of the state have always concentrated in the capital district itself in this decadal study, that is, 1991 to 2000.

The aspirations of the educated unemployed youth are reflected in their preferences and desires for particular jobs. These educated unemployed prefers government jobs to private and self-employed jobs, for government jobs promises stability and security of tenure with assured levels of wages and salaries along with guaranteed retirement benefits. Most of them do not like the hard manual work, but they want sedentary jobs and are inclined towards the desk job. Their first preferred choice is relatively for white-collar jobs. However, in case of no other alternative, majority of them are ready for even manual jobs. Therefore, the final aspiration of the educated unemployed youth is found to consist in getting any job in order to earn a livelihood.

The desire to 'acquire more knowledge' emerged as the primary reason for seeking education with all the faculties, for all occupational groups and also for all income groups. The study showed a great discrepancy between the occupational preferences and the occupational expectations. The difference between the two ranges a low of -33.51 percent and a high of +12.04 percent. For instance, 48.69 per cent of the educated unemployed youth preferred to be administrative officials, but only 15.18 per cent expected to get it resulting a wide discrepancy of -33.51 per cent.

The location of job is not the primary consideration for preference when there is scope for interesting work and security, higher salary. Yet preference for urban locations is slightly greater than rural areas. The study reveals that 88.48 per cent of the educated unemployed youth regard achievement criteria (education, hard work and ability) to be the most important factor for getting satisfactory jobs.

The study reveals that the future of the educated youth is expected to be very bleak in view of the shrinking employment opportunities. The proportion of the main workers to total population in the state is decreasing resulting to increase of unemployment among the educated. There is no balance between the number of students produced and the number of jobs available. The study reveals that most unemployed youth have remained without any remunerative job for 3 years and they blame the government for not getting a job. The average frequency of job attempts by these educated youth is twice and most respondents perceive that it will take another 5 more years for them to get any job. The perspective of job market looks gloomy, though many educated youth remains hopeful. And as a result the educated unemployed youth in the state are worried, very much worried about the prospect of employment.

Educated unemployed youth, despite inexhaustible energy and undefeatable enthusiasm appears to be a burden on their families and society. He is desperate for any kind of job but finds no one to buy him. He feels like a 'death sentence' or a poison has been put under his throat when somebody asks him "what are you doing now-a-days?" He finds himself answerable to the aspirations and expectations of the family. He is answerable to the family who has invested on him its sweat earned money with a hope that he will emancipate the family from all socio-economic curses after his education. The educated unemployed not only appear to be the victim of familial and social expectations, but also find himself guilty and faces humiliation.

The study reveals that the method of selection to various jobs is not appropriate as it is biased towards the rich and the bureaucrats. Corruption, nepotism, favouritism, tribalism, etc. in the process of selection is unanimously accepted by the respondents. It is agreed by most respondents that 'money and influence' has unfortunately become the formula to procure a job. This practice and formula by procuring a job has become the norm of the day. The governmental departments are blamed for improper notification of vacant jobs and for stagnation of development due to improper utilization of funds.

The educated unemployed youth attitude towards the Employment Exchange seems to be critical, as it seems no useful task than that of a 'notice board'. Most youth are of the view that it is not necessary to get registered to secure employment. The very purpose of the Exchange got defeated when all the vacant jobs are not notified through it, and the Employees are not bound to select out of those send through it. The common youth have lost faith in the Exchange when unfair treatment is usually done in forwarding the names against the notified vacancies. In the view of the youth, they should be provided 'unemployment allowances' if they are registered with the Exchange.

As against the general findings of many scholars, this study finds that the educated unemployed are satisfied with the quality of the present education system. The youth opines that university courses still prepare the students for jobs and therefore it is not a waste to give higher education to the youth even though there are no jobs available. The youth are satisfied with the English medium of instruction.

The educated unemployed youth are temperamentally frustrated, impatient, and restless. On account of unemployment he feels boredom and dullness, the feeling of self-contempt and self-distrust develops. He cannot keep self-respect and have the feeling that he is not well treated by his people. Unemployment has led to disorganization, disunity and discord among the family and it has disrupted peace with neighbours.

'Educated unemployed youth' is one of the vulnerable groups in society. The study reveals that unemployment among the educated has contributed to the spread of drugs and alcoholism, smuggling and drug-trafficking. Most of the respondents agree that due to unemployment, the educated youth are taking to anti-social activities like bandits, highway robberies, extortion, etc. The unemployed youth has become economically vulnerable; thereby they are increasingly getting into the trap of violence.

The agrarian occupation that supports more than 82.26 per cent of the total rural population has lost its status. The main reason for unwillingness (or secondary option) of the youth to work in farming sector is that it is not as productive when compared to other jobs.

Youth-hood in the state is subject to insecurity; therefore unemployed youth are more inclined towards government jobs rather than self-employment. Youth feel that the implementation of the various self-employment schemes operating in the state is not fair, and by and large, a complete failure. It also appears that the educated youth do not want to take any entrepreneurial risk involved in the self-employment, no entrepreneurial zeal and skill, and at the same time they do not allow outsiders to invest freely.

Optimism, energy and enthusiasm, merit and mission, aspirations and attempts receive a distinct set back when the educated youth fail to find adequate opportunities. This gulf between expectations and harsh realities leads to mounting disillusionment and frustration, anger and guilt. In a nutshell, the educated unemployed youth experience the following problems:

a) The educated youth appears to be in 'lost of trust' of the family for being unemployed.

b) The unemployed youth develops a feeling of frustration and distress, self-contempt, guilt and looses self-confidence on the non-fulfillment of his family expectations.

c) The unemployed youth fails to adjust with his friends, his family and the society.

d) The unemployed youth is dejected by the society and looses respect and sympathy of the people.

e) The unemployed youth feels deprived due to corruption, nepotism, favouritism and biased method of selection.

f) Due to overwhelming frustration and the feeling of worthlessness, it has often resulted into mal-nutrition and ill health of the youth.

g) The unemployed youth faces financial hardship.

h) The unemployed youth suffers from identity formation and as a result identifies oneself with symbols of a job.

The educated unemployed youth must be encouraged and their energies must be cultivated and channelized in order to make productive citizens. They should be motivated not to depend merely on government jobs that are scarce and difficult to get but certainly to achieve their goal by self-employment as one alternative. Self-employment programmes should be feasible and expanded. And the failures of self-employment schemes should be checked. A system of selection, proper training, and identification of trade/skills related to local economy, financial support, and marketing arrangements should be made and it should not be handicapped by the politics and the bureaucratic system of implementation.

The findings of the present study in accordance with the general findings of many scholars, is a very complex socio-economic phenomenon and its causation is multi-dimensional. The approach to its solution and efforts to remove obstacles would have to be multi-pronged and multi-phased covering not only the programmes for the educated unemployed youth but also the education system, and economic institutions.

This problem of unemployment among the educated youth is a serious problem, which needs timely attention and solution. Unemployment should not be viewed as a 'residual' problem to be tackled after the other problems have been solved, but as a 'primary' problem. Determined efforts are needed and appropriate policies, plans and programmes are to be made so that our young men and women can become job creators and not job seekers.

Bibliography

Agarwal, A.K: *Economic Problems and Planning in North East India;* New Delhi, Sterling Publishers Private Ltd. 1987.

Aggarwal, Suresh Chand and J.K.Goyal: "Trends in Youth Unemployment in India: An Empirical Analysis" in *The Indian Journal of Labour Economics;* Vol 43, No. 4, Oct-Dec, 2000.

Ahamad, B and M.Blaug (Ed): *The Practice of Manpower Forecasting;* New York, Elsevier Scientific Publishing Company, 1973.

Ahuja, Ram: *Social Problems in India (Second Edition);* New Delhi, Rawat Publications, 1997.

Aldcroft, Derek H: *Full Employment: The Exclusive Goal;* Great Britain, Wheatsheaf Books Ltd. 1984.

Atchly, Robert C: *The Social Forces in Later Life Miami Florida;* Scripts Foundation Grant Centre, Miami University, 1977.

Bairoch, Paul: *Urban Unemployment in Developing Countries;* International Labour Organisation, 1973.

Bajpai, Pramod Kumar: *Youth, Education and Unemployment;* New Delhi, Ashish Publishing House, 1992.

Behari, Bepin: *Unemployment, Technology and Rural Poverty;* New Delhi, Vikas Publishing House Pvt. Ltd. 1983.

Berger, P.L and B.Berger: *Sociology - A Biographical Approach;* New York, Basic Book Inc. 1972.

Bhalla, Sheela: "Trends in Poverty, Wages and Employment in India" in *The Indian Journal of Labour Economic;* Vol 40, April-June, 1997.

Bhat, C, Laxmi Narayan Kadikas and K.Ranga Rao (Ed): *Sociology of Development and Change;* New Delhi, Orient Longman Ltd.

1993.

Bhat, S.Ganesh: "Employment Generation through Entrepreneurship

Development" in *The Indian Journal of Labour Economics;* Vol 43, No. 4, 2000.

Bose, Nirmal Kumar: *Calcutta - A Social Survey;* Bombay, Lalvani Publishing House, 1968.

Chadha, G.K: "Youth Unemployment in India: Past Policy Gaps and Future Strategic Options" in *The Indian Journal of Labour Economics;* Vol 43, No. 4, Oct-Dec, 2000.

Chakrapani, C: *Unemployment Stress - A Study of Educated Unemployed;* New Delhi, Vikas Publishing House Pvt. Ltd. 1995.

Chaud, Mahesh: *Employment and Migration in Allahabad City;* Calcutta,Oxford & IBH Publishing Co. 1969.

Chauhan, S.S (Ed): *Advanced Educational Psychology;* New Delhi, Vikas Publishing House, 1990.

Colin, Murray Parkes: *Bereavement;* New York, International University Press, 1972.

Cullingworth, J.B: *Problems of an Urban Society (Vol I);* London, George Allen & Unwin Ltd. 1973.

Curran, Daniel J and Claire M.Renzetti: *Social Problems (Third Edition);* USA, 1993.

Das, Bhakta: *Unemployment in Assam, An Account of Human Error;* New Delhi, Cosmo Publications, 1992.

Dhar, T.N, A.S.Ilhman and W.F.Ilchman: *Education and Employment in India;* Calcutta, Minerva Associates (Publications) Pvt. Ltd. 1976.

Dholakia, Jitendra: *Unemployment and Employment Policy in India;* New Delhi, Sterling Publishers Pvt. Ltd. 1977.

Douglas, H.Powell and Paul F.Driscoll: "Middle Class Professional Face Unemployment" in *Society;* January-February, 1973.

D'Souza, Errol: "World Employment - 120 Perspective" in *Economic and Political Weekly;* Vol XXXIII, No. 39, Sept 26-Oct 2, 1998.

Dubey, Muchkund (Ed): *Indian Society Today: Challenges of Equality,Integration and Empowerment;* New Delhi, Har-Anand Publications, 1995.

Fernandes, Walter (Ed): *National Development and Tribal Deprivation;* New Delhi, Indian Social Institute, 1992.

Foster, Philip: *The Vocational School Fallacy in Development Planning: in Anderson, C.Arnold and M.J.Bowman (Eds.) - Education and Economic Development;* Chicago, Aldine, 1963.

Friedman, F.G: *Society and Youth;* London, MacMillan, 1971.

Gill, Sucha Singh: "Educated Unemployment in Punjab" in *The Indian Journal of Labour Economics;* Vol 43, No. 4, Oct-Dec, 2000.

Godfrey, Martin: *Global Unemployment - the New Challenges for Economic Theory;* UK, Harverter Press 1986.

Goode, William J and Paul K Hatt: *Methods in Social Research;* New York, McGraw Hill Book Company, 1952.

Green, A.W: *Sociology;* New York, MacMillan Press, 1956.

Hannington, Wal: *Unemployed struggles 1919 - 1936;* London, Lawrence and Wishant Ltd. 1979.

Hashim, S.R: "Employment and Poverty - Some Emerging Policy Issues" in *The Indian Journal of Labour Economics;* Vol 42, No. 1, Jan-Mar, 1999.

Hiramani, A.B and Nulam Sharma (Ed): *Health and Youth in India;* Delhi, Agam Prakashan, 1988.

Hoda, Mansur: *Problems of Unemployment in India;* Bombay, Allied Publishers Pvt. Ltd. 1974.

Jahoda, Marie, Paul F.Lazarsfeld and Hans Zeisel: *Marienthal: The Sociography of an Unemployed Community;* Great Britain, Tawistock Publications, 1972.

Johnson, Gloria Jones and W.Roy Johnson: "Subjective Underemployment and Job Satisfaction" in *International Review of Modern Sociology;* Vol 25 (Spring), No.1, 1995.

Krishna, Raj: "Unemployment in India" in *Economic and Political Weekly;* Vol VIII, No. 9, Mar 3, 1973.

Kuppuswammy B (Ed): *Advanced Educational Psychology;* New Delhi, Sterling Publishers Pvt. Ltd. 1984.

Lapang, D.D: "Tap Resources to Generate Jobs - Growing Unemployment causing much Frustration among Youths in the Sate" in *The Meghalaya Guardian;* May 13, 1999.

Leonor, M.D (Ed): *Unemployment, Schooling & Training in Developing Countries;* London, Croom Helm, 1985.

MacIver, R.M and Page, C.H: *Society: An Introductory Analysis;* London, MacMillan, 1959.

Mahalanobis, P.C: *Papers on Planning (Ed. P.K.Bose & M.Mukherjee);* Calcutta, Statistical Publishing Society, 1985.

Mali, D.D: *Economic Problems and Planning in Assam;* New Delhi, Omsons Publications, 1989.

Malinvaud, Edmond: *Mass Unemployment;* London, Basil Blackwell Publishers Ltd. 1984.

Mamoria, C.B and S.Mamoria: *Marketing Management (Eleventh Edition);* Allahabad, Kitab Mahal Agencies, 1997.

Masum, Muhammad: *Unemployment and Under-Employment in Agriculture: A Case Study of Bangladesh;* B.R.Publishing Corporation, 1982.

Monly, J and E.Casta: *Employment Policies in Developing Countries (Ed. P.Lamartine Yates);* London, George Allen & Unwin Ltd. 1974.

Naba, Gopal Das: *Employment, Unemployment and Full Employment in India;* 1968.

Puttaswamaiah, K: *Unemployment in India -Policy for Manpower;* New Delhi, Oxford & IBH Publishing Co. 1977.

Raghavan, K and Leena Sekhar: *Poverty and Employment;* New Delhi, New Age International (P) Ltd. Publishers, 1996.

Rao, V.K.R.V (Ed): *Employment and Unemployment;* New Delhi, Allied Publishers Pvt. Ltd. 1968.

Ray, B.Datta (Ed): *Social and Economic Profile of North-East India;* New Delhi, B.R.Publishing Corporation, 1978.

Ray, P.K: "Employment, Unemployment and Under-Employment - An Analysis" in *The Indian Journal of Labour Economics;* Vol 41, No. 2, April-June, 1998.

Sattinger, Michael: *Unemployment, Choice and Inequality;* Springer-Verlag Berlin Heidelberg, 1985.

Saraswathi, S: *Youth in India;* New Delhi, Indian Council of Social Science Research, 1988.

Sen, A: *Employment, Technology and Development;* London, Oxford, 1975.

Sinclair, Peter: *Unemployment, Economic Theory and Evidence;* Oxford, Basil Blackwell Ltd. 1987.

Sunny, Dolly: "Unemployment and Employment of Educated Youth in Kerala" in *The Indian Journal of Labour Economics;* Vol 43, No. 4, Oct-Dec, 2000.

Taylor, Jim: *Unemployment and Wage Inflation - with Special Reference to Britain and USA;* London, Longman Group Ltd. 1975.

Temsu, L: *Job Aspiration among Youth in Mokokchung Town, Nagaland;* Dissertation, M.Phil, Deptt. of Sociology, NEHU, 1997.

Thakur, Dalip S: *Poverty, Inequality and Unemployment in Rural India;* Delhi, B.R.Publishing Corporation, 1985.

Thakur, Devendra and D.N.Thakur (Ed): *Tribal Labour and Employment (Tribal Life in India - 5);* New Delhi, Deep & Deep Publication, 1994.

Uppal, J.S: *Disguised Unemployment in an Underdeveloped Economy;* New Delhi, Asia Publishing House, 1973.

Young, Pauline V: *Scientific Social Surveys and Research (Fourth Edition);* New Delhi, Prentice Hall of India, 1996.

Young, Pauline V: "Employment and Unemployment" in *International Encyclopaedia of the Social Sciences;* Vol 5 and 6, MacMillan & Free Press, New York, 1972.

Young, Pauline V: "Employment Perspective: Documentation" in *The Indian Journal of Labour Economics;* Vol 42, No. 1, Jan-Mar, 1999.

Young, Pauline V: "Interstate Variations in Rural Unemployment Rates in India" in *Monthly Public Opinion Surveys;* Vol XLIII, No. 9, June, 1998.

Young, Pauline V: "Unemployment and Poverty" in *International Encyclopaedia of Sociology;* Vol 2, 1995.

Government of Nagaland, Directorate of Information and Public Relations, *Basic Facts: Nagaland (1997, 1998);* Kohima.

Government of Nagaland, Directorate of Tourism, *Nagaland Tourism (1998);* Kohima.

Government of Nagaland, Directorate of Economics and Statistics, *Statistical Hand Book of Nagaland (1996, 1997, 2000);* Kohima.

Index